Becoming Magic

Becoming Magic

A Path *of* Personal Reconstruction

ANTUAN MAGIC RAIMONE

TABLE OF CONTENTS

ACKNOWLEDGEMENTS

There are so many people who will not see themselves listed here and it's not because you aren't important to me; it's because I could not possibly list all of you without forgetting someone. To those who aren't listed, you have contributed just as much as those who are and I'm sure several of you will give me shit for not listing you, which will come as no surprise to me. ;)

I'd like to first acknowledge the voice in me that wanted to be heard. You were kept quiet for so long, by others and by me, out of fear. The people pleaser in me still gets scared about what you have to say, so I walk in faith that whatever it is will come from a place of love. I'd also like to acknowledge everyone that contributed to this book, either with your words, time or by being in my life.

To Momma, Rhon and Rob, thank you for growing towards me. There are many different ways our relationships could have gone and I'm thankful for where they are. You each have survived more than what I already know and more than I think I could. I appreciate your vulnerability as much as I do your strength.

Sis, thank you for holding my heart each time I don't have the strength to.

Kittie, I honestly can't imagine what my professional life would be without your theatre program, your friendship and your love. Thank you.

Neil, your light cannot be ignored and it's what both scared and drew me to you. You are "living proof" that when we shine, we give others permission to do the same.

To my "CARE" group, THANK YOU, THANK YOU, THANK YOU! My love and appreciation for you can't be fully expressed in words.

Alabanza to my Coquito Quad, you're the "showmance" that just won't end and I don't want it to.

Candi...WE DID IT!

Daddy-O, you aren't physically here to experience this with me, and I am confident your spirit and memory are ever present. You were my first hero and villain, which allowed me to see you as the human you were, and in your human form is where I was able to most fully love and appreciate you. You lived with so many quiet fears and I'm thankful I was able to help you release some of them.

To Amie, Christopher and the CVTC, your services changed, saved and brought a purpose to my life that I didn't know was waiting for me. For as long as I live, I will do what I can to show you my gratitude.

Mike, your love for me is probably as close to what I could have asked for, without knowing how it would look. It scares me at times. I'm scared I'll fuck it up or that I won't be enough. What I know is that I can share those fears with you, you'll hear them, and we'll figure something out together.

To the reader. Thank you for offering your time and money to take in my story. You didn't have to, and I'm humbled that you did. In reading this, I want you to see yourself reflected in me. See the artist in you, the child of a single parent, the little black boy, the survivor, the only one in the room who looks like you, the person in a small town dreaming of a bigger future, the LGBTQIA+ person finding yourself, the person who's afraid, who's courageous, who's silly. Lastly, I want you to see that YOU ARE LOVE AND YOU ARE LOVED. May this find you in good health and spirits.

INTRODUCTION

When the World Stopped Moving

"The moment is everything. Don't think about tomorrow; don't think about yesterday: think about exactly what you're doing right now and live it and dance it and breathe it and be it."
—WENDY WHELAN

"BROADWAY IS SHUT down until 2021."

Did we wake up to a new reality? One without music, art, expression...*dance*? Not possible. I would need to put an eye mask back on and go beddy-bye again.

The real story: Broadway theatres did abruptly close on March 12, 2020, knocking out all shows—including sixteen that were already scheduled to close soon. This announcement came months after Broadway, my second home, grossed $1.8 billion the previous season and attracted a record 15 million people. Much due to *Hamilton*, no doubt.

Fortunately, for me, as a universal swing, this is what I know the theatre industry to be. Every show stops at some point and when the show ends, I am unemployed. I knew my contract was coming up, and I wasn't sure if I was going to sign another contract or even get one. I entered this pandemic of the coronavirus with a decent nest egg, aspiring to fulfill other aspirations and spend more time with my boyfriend, as basic as that might sound. You see, I've been with *Hamilton* for three glorious, mind-blowing, heart-pounding years. My personal track record has been when work stops, the universe is presenting me with an opportunity or more emotional growth. It has opened up time for other creative endeavors, like this book and public speaking, that I wouldn't have been able to do among a normal show schedule. I was comforting a fellow performer acknowledging that there can be discomfort and pain in this process, but I trust it. I have faith in what I pour my heart into. I hope I inspired her.

Change can't be stopped, no matter what we do. Sometimes we may be able to prepare for it and other times, it will sneak up on us like a mosquito. In my case, it came like a mosquito bite.

On January 6, 2020, I flew home to New York after spending all of 2019 in Chicago for work. Getting back into the rhythm of being home was a bigger adjustment than I thought it would be. Just getting to work went from a seven-minute walk in Chicago to a forty-minute commute in New York. I'd forgotten how much time I spent out of my home when I was in New York. It's very common to leave my apartment around noon and not get back for almost twelve hours. And in those twelve hours I'm surrounded by people almost every step of the way, from my walk to the train, the train ride into Times Square, and my walk to the theatre. Then I breeze into the theatre where I share a dressing room with up to eight other people. On an average day, the only time I'll have to myself is when I use the single-occupancy bathroom outside of the dressing room.

I had been home for a little more than a week when my supervisor asked me to meet him before a Wednesday matinee. We hadn't spoken face-to-face in months, and he wanted to talk to me about some changes that were going to be happening with the universal swings of *Hamilton*.

My job as a universal swing is solely to commute around the country as needed to act in the various productions of *Hamilton*. He went on to tell me that I was going to be sent to one of the touring companies of the show that was currently in Florida. He wasn't able to tell me exactly how long I'd be on tour, but it was looking like a minimum of two months. There's that mosquito I mentioned earlier.

I did my best to hide my disappointment because it's my job to travel when I'm needed, and I was needed. It still bit me in the heart. I hadn't been home two weeks and had only seen my boyfriend twice in that time. He happened to be on a trip with some friends when I got the news I'd be leaving. I'd have four days before boarding a plane to Florida, but before that would happen, I would need to pack, do an afternoon rehearsal for the show in New York, perform two different parts in the course of two different days and spend time with my boyfriend once he got back from his trip. There was a lot to do in a short amount of time.

I was stunned. I hadn't fully processed leaving Chicago, a place that had been my home for over a year, and newly getting re-acclimated to my life back in New York to now have to switch gears to go to a city I'd never been to and work with a company of people I'd never met before. I don't know how anyone could handle that gracefully, myself included, and I was trying. Am I ungrateful for my job? Not in the least. Am I finding it hard to keep rolling with the ever-changing tide that keeps coming? Absolutely! There have been days when I've felt overwhelmed and wanted to scream for the world to stop moving, but I know it won't. Instead, I stop, take deep breaths and give myself one task to focus on. Once I've done all I can for that task, I move to the next one. I also listen to music. It's much more enjoyable to hear than the running lists I have clanging around in my head like pots and pans. I also ask others for help.

As my departure got closer, I knew I was going to need a mental health day from work, so I asked for it and got it. I spent my last day in New York with my boyfriend, at my apartment. It might not have been as much as I wanted, but it was at least what I needed.

As I mentioned before, change can't be stopped and can be a disruptor. Change can also be an opportunity for us to grow. It can offer us the chance to speak up for ourselves and ask for what we need. If you find yourself overwhelmed by changes in your life, be it personal or professional, take time to ask yourself, "What do I need now?" Do you need to take time for a walk, to call a friend and talk out what you're going through, or take a hot shower or soak in a bath? What is something you can do for you? No one else will give you what you need until you ask for it, and that goes for asking yourself as well. And there may be surprises around the corner. Like an unprecedented global theatre shutdown!

Over the months since the coronavirus made itself known, the world has transformed and there is no binary way to describe it. What I will say is that it's overwhelming. For everyone. There was a time when many of us didn't have to think about what our day-to-day looked like. Whether we saw the day ahead of us as good or bad, we knew that there was a particular routine in front of us. Now we are in new routines in which going to the store is not an absent-minded act anymore. Before I walk out of my apartment to do anything, I put on my face mask, grab a pair of rubber gloves and make sure I have hand sanitizer. I also find that in addition to putting on a face mask and disposable gloves, I'm wearing fear. It's not an accessory I like having with me.

The first week of April 2020 was a turning point for me. My consciousness rippled out a little further from my personal shore of comfort and it shook me. On one hand I was safe in my apartment, which I call my "earth haven." My apartment marked my financial independence and is the first home I've put time, energy, money and love into, in a way that only I could. It's also where I've longed to be for more than a year due to being away for work. A pandemic is far from what I thought would bring me home and yet, I am so utterly grateful to be here. I am financially secure, even though I have no idea when I'll return to work. I'm in good health and mostly in good spirits, depending on the day. On the other hand, as I watch the news each day, I see how widely this virus is infecting and affecting so many of us in ways that extend far beyond our health. At times, it has made my spirit weary. My spirit is weary for my friends that have no idea how they will be able to pay their bills. Weary for my friends who are actors that are seeing months of income, healthcare, insurance and artistic expression being wiped off the calendar with every passing week, in a career that is already fragile by nature. I'm also weary for every life that has and will be lost because of this powerful and indiscriminate virus. I'm weary for the various service providers that make the conscious decision to jeopardize not just their own health but also, the health of their loved ones, every time they go to work.

Something I am re-discovering for myself during this time of isolation and introspection is that I can function in more than one state of emotion at a time. Even with my best attempts to limit the weight of fear I feel each day, there are days when my ability to keep fear at a distance doesn't work. I started working on this book under the unavoidable weight of fear. As I've worked on it, love becomes more present. I think that's because I'm allowing myself to *embrace* where I am. I use the word "embrace" in a very conscious way. I am not resigned or surrendering from a place of hopelessness; it's quite the opposite. By embracing my ever-changing emotional state, without judgement, I am, in fact, responding from a place of love. There are many ways to embrace fear in a way that will keep you physically and emotionally healthy. It all starts with recognizing when fear is present. I've sat alone in my apartment crying or I've put music on and danced alone. I've taken a drive two hours out of New York City with my boyfriend, and I've also spent a full day watching television from the comfort of my bed. Fear needs as much space, attention and nurturing as love does, and my experience has shown me that when I allow fear the space it needs, love follows closely behind.

Is fear pulling at you, asking to be seen, heard or felt? If your answer is yes, how are you embracing it? If your answer is no, is there a way you could embrace it? There is no wrong answer to these questions, only an opportunity for us to find a deeper connection with ourselves. I had a lengthy relationship with fear that would put Lady Gaga's bad romance to shame! But fear can be a friend…kind of like that messy, lovable friend that has bad manners but good intentions and infectious laughter. Befriending fear requires a full emotional excavation and knowing what, of your emotional palette, to let go of. Letting go is not easy by any means; however, it is possible.

We all have our own emotional history that has shaped how we see the world and certain situations in our lives. This may sound radical (as if living through a pandemic isn't radical!), but I would like to encourage you to let go of that history. Emotional history is outdated and limited because we are not the same people today that we were then. Through learning of my story, you will see that I'm an expert on this. At that time in the past, we were working from a different skill set emotionally and unless we have chosen to stunt our emotional growth, we continue to have a wider, accessible emotional skill set to work from. I'm not saying that it isn't helpful to learn from our emotional pasts. We just don't have to live today as if it were the same as five, twenty or forty years ago. And if it is the same, why are we choosing to keep it the same?

I would like to show you what it's like to Become Magic. I invite you to be a personal champion for yourself. I'm not asking you to emulate and replicate. I would like for you to be inspired to draw from my story for yourself. A "Path of Personal Reconstruction" is not only a statement that I am declaring here; it's also a query for you.

CHAPTER 1

Six Men, Five Cities

"Pride, envy, avarice—the sparks that have
set on fire the hearts of all men."

—DANTE ALIGHIERI

I WAS BORN Antuan Raimone Budgett. Once I decided on a career in theatre, I started thinking about what my professional name would be. "Budgett" seemed sharp and short. I decided to go with Antuan Raimone for my professional name in 1998. Then in 2007, Magic was given to me.

In 2007, I was hired as the vacation swing for the Off-Broadway production of *In the Heights*, working with the two dance captains, Michael Balderrama ("Baldy") and Stephanie Klemons. Baldy was teaching me the show. I have an insane ability to watch choreography and pick up the details and nuances very quickly. I always had an ability for memory and spatial awareness and assumed that other people did. I could probably tell you exactly how far my closet is from where I am standing. That also comes with my habitual pattern of putting everything back to where I retrieved it from. Everything has its place and there will never be a question where it is. As Baldy taught the show, he would teach me something and I would get it and ask, "What's next?"

We were scheduled for a four-hour rehearsal once, but it ended up being an hour because there was an emergency at the theatre, and he was needed. Next day, when I came in, he asked me to show him what I could remember from the night before, and it was the whole teaching despite our squeezed time. When cast members would ask him how the new guy was, he said, splendid. "He picks it up just like that. Like magic!" He has called me that ever since. It took some time, but I would eventually embrace the name, putting me into a kind of questionable spotlight for a calm and unassuming guy. To get that kind of nickname from Baldy, whose career includes productions like Michael Jackson's *Ghost*, *In the Heights*, *Hot Feet*, *Movin' Out*, *Urban Cowboy*, and *Saturday Night Fever*, and has worked with Gloria Estefan, Bruno Mars, Sutton Foster, Vanessa Williams, Brian Adams, Mariah Carey—respect!

How could I not become Magic?

J. Philip Bassett ("JB"), a stage manager on Broadway for more than two decades, can vouch for me: "He learned tracks as a swing faster than anybody I've known. He could understand something in the first pass and all-consuming and manifest it like nobody else. Magic."

So, I started introducing myself as Magic, but I would always have this weird glitch in my intros to people. I felt arrogant saying Magic, but in the performance world, it was more acceptable. I stopped being so embarrassed about introducing myself as Magic. It was unofficially part of my professional name. And I swear, like magic, I started seeing certain instances of life as magic, too. Like dancing my ass off for a role in *Hamilton* and getting it.

JB, the original stage manager, describes the picture of what being a part of this production signified: "Everybody believed it would be a big hit. No one knew how big. I got hired in March of 2015 and tickets went on sale shortly after that. I was close to the management office. For a show to sell $1 million makes it a massive hit, but *Hamilton* blew that out of the water. Tens of millions of dollars a day. Something that no one had experienced in that volume of ticket sales. So, what could it be compared to? *Wicked*? *Book of Mormon*? When it did that kind of business in the first day, it indicated it would be bigger than anything including *Rent*, things that are massive. It launched into a category by itself. We didn't know what to brace for. The only thing you could do is tuck your head, do the work. We went to work mounting the show and ultimately, you only have so many seats to sell. You don't have more seats. Every seat, every night. Full house every night and you don't have to ask that question. You ask this for other shows because if a show has half a house, you want to prepare your performers so if they walk out on stage and only see half full, they're not thrown or shocked by it. We could assume a full house for as long as we ran the show.

"In the first week of previews, Barack Obama wanted to come in two days. We instantly had Secret Service in the building. We hadn't even opened the show and were still refining it. We needed to have interviews with Secret Service, figure out a command center for the President, and have snipers on the roof! On top of everything we had to accomplish. With *Hamilton*, many of the things are already mind-blowing. So, you can revel in the bizarre world you're in later. Let's 'get it done' first. And we did, to rave reviews. We sold out for a year, so we didn't have to deal with the logistics of performing on *Good Morning America*, *Today*, *Late Night*. That was the right decision. Then the Grammy Awards wanted a show and we said we would do it remotely. At first, they said 'no', and we refused so they came back. It was an indicator to how unique the show is and the kind of clout it has. The only other time they took a virtual show was Madonna in the nineties."

Every aspect of this show had meaning. It's even difficult for me to simply call *Hamilton* a show, because I've done many "shows." *Hamilton* is more like a phenomenon.

JB recalls me breaking down in tears after the first dress rehearsal in Chicago. I was sitting in the mezzanine as a part of a family that was in their creative light and gainfully employed in the cutting edge of theatre that would be taken in by 2.6 million over the course of 2,000 performances (pre-Disney broadcasting, at that). There was something about my life that had come full circle and landed on that moment.

So much happened in such a short time. Barack Obama being dazzled by the show was one thing, but then Donald J. Trump got elected as U.S. President. The Chicago show had just opened a month before, and JB happened to be there on Election Day. It was grim, even devastating. Tommy, the director, encouraged him to remind the performers that the moment was a time for activism. The show is by itself an active revolution. The show morphed in front of his face because it was born under Barack Obama with so much joy and pride and then Trump got elected. And different lyrics, different moves occurred. I imagine it will do that forever. *Hamilton* is so all-encompassing about politics that it will change with the leader sitting in the Oval Office.

We had Broadway. We were going to open Chicago, then London. JB's strategy was to hire a bunch of performers that were "strictly *Hamilton*." In 2016, no one knew what it was unless they had seen it on Broadway. Word of mouth was it. The album had not been released so performers didn't know what they were walking into. They couldn't prepare in advance, so it became a complicated process. JB and Stephanie sat down to discuss this idea of a universal swing. Someone who could go from Broadway to Chicago or to the tour.

A male and female swing would be needed to cover the ensemble, which included five women and six men. When you add different companies, one would think each *Hamilton* would be a carbon copy of the last, but our music supervisor and choreographer didn't want to be held to that. Essentially, Man 3 in Chicago could be more of Man 2 on Broadway with a little of 4 sprinkled in, so hiring a universal swing, Broadway to Chicago, meant learning twelve different tracks that could translate from one show to the next.

He adds: "It seemed obvious that Magic was going to be one of our go-to people because of this extraordinary talent he has to do just that for this kind of role. And let alone, eighteen different tracks if we decided to put him on tour. It meant ability to adapt seamlessly and quickly so they could float amongst companies. Being a swing is challenging enough. Some people tap out after the six! Even finding a swing is a needle in the haystack. But finding someone with Magic's ability is one in a million. Sixty percent become very good swings, but 30 percent can't keep up to speed, then another 10 or 15 percent tap out. Nobody faults anyone for that because some brains don't work like that. It's better to know before you hire someone and spend money on costumes, rehearsals, but sometimes that is not possible. Knowing we would make this kind of investment into a person, knowing Magic, made it absolute."

Who doesn't want to be known as absolute? It would be my highest honor.

You hear people say that it helps to know someone in this business (or who to sleep with!), but I don't think of this in the way that you think. I'm referring to the bond you make as a chosen family and helping to ensure each other's future in the industry.

Amber White was in her twenties when we met during *In the Heights*, where she was assistant stage manager. We became fast friends. For a stage manager, so much of the job is to collaborate with artists to figure out how to help them do their art and perform eight times a week or stay fresh. Keep the show consistent and clean and not drill down so they don't feel boxed in. They have to work collectively with everyone because ultimately, you have deadlines and schedules. Cohesion is part of the job. That's Amber's current stage manager's job description. They call the show, make sure backstage runs smoothly, and put out a schedule. Then there is the long-term management to keep a show going.

Imagine my elation to see that JB and Amber would be on the stage management team of *Hamilton*. She was also seven months pregnant in the run-up to the show. She was set to give birth the day before *Hamilton* started to rehearse. Five months after her beautiful daughter was born, she moved into production supervisor right away. We've developed a deep bond, and we often compare our personal lives with our performance lives. If you could set certain events to music, I'm sure Amber and I would come up with the best playlist!

In her words: "Magic has been able to look within and take that long-term journey of life to turn adversities inside out and use them as a positive experience. That ability is so unique because it's hard. It's not something everyone can do. Between *Heights* and *Hamilton*, I saw him do this. A path of personal reconstruction. When he was at the point of talking about this out loud, that was a beautiful thing to see. The time that he was with us in New York, I loved hearing what he was up to. It escalated quickly with his TEDx Talk. He got noticed and that encourages you to continue. He's still quiet and calculated, but you can tell that calculation is about bringing something out. What he does as a performer is similar to who he is as a person. He takes the information, and something is happening, then you just have a performance."

They also hired the extremely gifted Eliza Ohman, who I had danced alongside in the ensemble of *Radio City Christmas Spectacular*. We were the first universal swings that *Hamilton* hired. We call each other "Swing Star." If she says it, I agree without a second thought. That is how much I trust her. Our brains have unique wiring.

Eliza recalls of our bond: "Magic was my lifeline at *Hamilton*. Those first three months of learning the show were chaotic! I was terrified every single day, but *especially* on the first day of rehearsal. I was swinging, which I'd never done before, and on day one, my male counterpart hadn't been hired. I really felt like I was going it alone. The next day, I sat in my seat feeling completely isolated from the company and saw Magic's name on the binder next to mine. Everything felt safer. My male counterpart was Magic. A ray of sunshine, the person that demonstrated to me the value of using my voice (which I definitely needed those first few months), and someone who'd done this before. Whenever we rehearsed the show with the other swings, Magic was my partner. I learned the show with his body and his energy. We didn't get a chance to partner together onstage for almost a year. By that point, I'd partnered with almost a dozen of the men in the company but sharing the stage with him felt like home. For the first time I felt like I was performing the show I learned, not because my other partners hadn't been great, but they weren't my first introduction to the world."

What a world!

It is a world I would navigate for three years. My job is to know everything that the male ensemble/chorus has to do in the show…for five different companies. To be more specific, I have to know the differences in choreography, vocal parts, blocking, set moves, prop moves and costume changes for SIX MEN IN FIVE DIFFERENT CITIES. Imagine if you had to know every detail for six of your coworkers and you could be asked to do someone else's job at a moment's notice. Sounds impossible, maybe even ridiculous and it's been my every day for three years. And I love it! It keeps the show fresh for me because I get to see it from a different angle each time that I'm on stage and my body gets a rest by not having to perform every night. It also means that I can be away from home for weeks, and as the case was in 2019, months, at a time.

I confess, I engaged in a lot of conversations with dear friends and colleagues in order to help me put the pieces of my life together for your reading pleasure. But it is hard to express just how pinpoint-accurate others' views and recollections of me are. It is shocking and affirming to hear about snippets of your life. It also shows the totality and power of perception and empathy. Humanity. They relayed my life, the whole tapestry of agony and ecstasy, far better than I could alone. Particularly my maturity from silence to my own version of loudness.

Swing Star says of a very pivotal part of my life in 2014 when we had met in *Radio City Christmas Spectacular*. "Throughout the rehearsal process I was so grateful to him because as someone only a year into my career, I didn't always feel empowered to use my voice, but Antuan set the example that asking questions, saying what you need, and advocating for yourself is the only way forward professionally. That mindset may not work in all spaces, but if it doesn't, I know now those aren't my spaces! Since meeting Antuan I've watched him grow most significantly in his emotional health. When we met, he was processing his father's passing and still processing a lot of shame he carried with him since he was a young boy. Each year, I watched him grow more certain that other people's narratives about him had no bearing over the life he'd choose to lead. Societal conformity that didn't serve him would no longer define him or influence him."

CHAPTER 2

Growing Up with Shadow Figures

*"If you know the enemy and know yourself you need
not fear the results of a hundred battles."*

—Sun Tzu

I ALWAYS LOVED to dance when I was a kid and sang in my church
choir, first as an alto and then a tenor. At any kind of family event, I
could be found dancing. I was naturally flexible and could do center,
left and right splits without thinking about it. I would watch music
videos and learn the choreography by watching it over and over again.
In high school, my alarm clock was the radio. In sum, I listened to—
and lived—music nonstop.

I am from Blue Springs, Missouri, about twenty-five minutes east of
Kansas City and over four hours from Ferguson. When I was a kid, the
population was between 17,000 and 21,000. According to my mother, I
was easier to raise compared to my two older, more vocal sisters. I didn't
like being punished so it didn't take much to keep me in line.

Our mother was a single mom for the most part, a sole provider while my father gave her grief, so Rhonda and Robin had a lot of responsibilities when I came into their world. Rhonda was going on sixteen years old and about to set the fashion industry on fire. Back in the 1960s, if you saw an African American man in Macy's and JC Penney's catalogs and Hallmark cards, that was my sisters' dad as the first. Hallmark Cards needed children and they didn't have any African American children, so they asked him if Rhonda and Robin could be a part of the brand and do Easter and Christmas cards. My sisters became the first African American children to be on a Hallmark card. In doing that, it was an instant talent, particularly for Rhonda. She also played the piano and clarinet and sang in the choir. An introvert by nature, Rhonda enrolled in a talent agency's class for confidence. She wanted to get into broadcasting. The scout pushed her to become a model.

As if being the ethnic face of Hallmark weren't bold enough, Rhonda was the first African American student to go to Europe to do couture and prêt-à-porter modeling for commercials and catalogs. Then she entered AFTC, where talent from around the world was scouted by agents and producers. And here is where the road to fame got windy for Rhonda. They were doing a swimsuit contest and they wanted her to change, but she was very shy, and she never believed in showing her body, at least publicly. This woman cajoled her friend to take Rhonda upstairs to get dressed. She was crying! By the time she changed and got back downstairs, they were getting ready to call her name—to walk in front of 2,000 people. Well, my big sis got through the whole event and at the gala, they announced awards. She had won "overall model" for her division among several awards. That night changed Rhonda's life. This scout saw something in her that she didn't know she had, which propelled her career. Three weeks later, at a fashion show, an agent asked Rhonda if she was ready to move to Paris to start her career. Blue Springs to Paris! She paved the way, announcing to her siblings that there was no limit.

In the meantime, Robin took care of me the best she could. She was thrilled to have a baby brother and showed it every chance she got.

When she hung out with friends, I was still sitting in a stroller at her hip. I remember one summer day, them hanging out and me getting in the stroller. She pushed me while she talked to her friend. I love that memory. Robin gave me a Betty Boop T-shirt that she couldn't wear anymore and I'm not ashamed to share that I obsessively started to collect Betty paraphernalia because of that connection with Robin. She didn't hit the runway, but she is immensely talented, too. She may regret not getting into entertainment because she would have been a success. However, she retired as a chief in the U.S. Navy and has gone on to get her bachelor's degree, in addition to being a mother of five remarkable women.

My mother raised us all with music around the house but had no clue about the business of entertainment or what opportunities lurked for us. She worked very hard, holding sometimes two or three jobs, and she pressed us to have good grades. That was the basic criteria repeated over and over in the household. As I got old enough to understand the game, I observed the systems that Rhonda and Robin created in order to get what they wanted from Mom. I learned a thing or two.

Rhonda explains, "I learned to have a plan before talking to her. If I wanted something to happen, I needed to have a full explanation first. We all needed to have this approach. All she had to do was sit and wait for our results! My dad understood fashion and entertainment. My mom went through a lot with Antuan's father. She was very controlling, which meant she was out of control sometimes. God gave me the wisdom to learn how to deal with her. I told my siblings that we always had to honor our parents and we would live a long life. I've always had a connection with God. We don't get to pick our parents."

My sisters went to these faraway places and my mother was supportive of it. Because I had that blueprint from them, it made it easier for me to leave home, go to college, travel on cruise ships, and move to New York. I had this innate feeling that Mom would be okay if I did anything even close to this.

Much of my childhood existed with my father out of that picture.

In my memory, I can only recall us living together as a family for maybe four years of my childhood. For a long time, I was mad at my dad for not being there and even went so far as to not care if he was or not; I became indifferent about it. I have a close friend that says indifference is worse than hate or anger because with hate or anger you have at least connected an emotion to that person.

Over the years, I have learned to forgive my father. What I now know is that my dad, whom I call "Daddy-O," was doing the best he knew how to do when he knew it. He would grow exponentially over the years, and so have I. We grew individually and also together as father and son. He missed so many birthdays and performances, either because I didn't invite him, or he just didn't come to them. He didn't teach me to shave, tie a tie, or even how to drive. The most important thing he did, however, was tell me he loved me and was proud of me every time I talked to him. He was also an affectionate man, hugging me whenever we got together; such important elements of our relationship I will always remember.

His absence when I was a child certainly contributed to my loneliness and sense of never fitting in as a child.

I was very aware of other people's moods. That came from me being aware of my mother's mood at home. It was a regular occurrence for her to be frustrated with work, with my father and their relationship. Somewhere along the way, I became a very observant kid. I needed to know how I fit in. How do I not make things worse? I started learning how to insert myself in social situations like this. Waiting to see what a group wanted to do or how they acted. Because of this, I didn't develop my own voice as a kid.

The best thing that happened to me as a child was meeting the pretty, vivacious and best bubblegum-smackin' Danica ("Sis") at six years old, and maybe within a few minutes, we were each other's first boyfriend and girlfriend. We were two of the only children of color at our school, so we connected on numerous levels. Four months into the school year, my buddy moved away. We kept in touch as much as six-year-olds could stay in contact, but her absence left a gaping hole in my heart and my little universe.

At the age of eight, I was sexually abused by two members of my extended family. When it all started, I thought that we were playing a game. They were brothers and since I'm the only boy of three siblings, I thought that what we were going to do was something brothers did together. I also wanted to fit in. The only boys that I had in my life at that time were the other boys that lived on my block, or the ones I went to school with. I wasn't as rough and tumble as them and I wasn't uncomfortable being around girls. I didn't like sports the same way other boys did either. I didn't even watch them at home. In so many ways, I felt out of place and wanted to be included. My family was the only family of color in our neighborhood, my mother was a single parent working as much as she could to make ends meet and I didn't spend much time with my dad. Being able to spend time with not only other boys, but also, boys that were my family, was something I'd wanted for a long time, or so I thought.

It was the summer, and I would spend the weekend with them at their mom's apartment. The oldest of us was maybe twelve, with the younger brother being my same age of eight. Their mother, my aunt, would leave for work and we were given strict instructions not to answer the door for anybody and to call her if we needed anything. Shortly after she left, the oldest, "D," would tell us to take off our pajamas. We were in their room and standing in our underwear and I seemed to be the only one that had no idea what was going on. I'd never been with other boys in my under-wear before and I followed along because again I wanted to fit in. "D" would instruct me to lay stomach down, on the bed. He was the oldest, so I followed. He would then tell his brother, "A," to lay on top of me and then he laid on top of "A." Something inside of me knew that what was happening wasn't right and I ignored it. Every alarm that fired off in the cells of my body commanded me not to go along with this, but what was I supposed to do? I was trapped in that apartment and trapped under the weight of their bodies. If I called my mom and asked her to pick me up early, she'd ask why. I would have been too scared to tell her. I didn't live close enough to walk home, even if I wanted to.

There is so much about that weekend that I have forgotten and will never remember, but there is one image branded in my brain. As I laid there, afraid and frozen, I left my body. In my memory of that day, I can see my eight-year-old self staring blankly out. He doesn't make a sound and he doesn't cry. He doesn't fight. No movement. He waits. He waits for it to be over.

I won't speak about what happened to me to anyone for at least a decade and unfortunately, that secret won't be the only one I have to keep.

One happy report of that era was that Sis and her family moved back to the same cul-de-sac in the same development we met in. She was roller skating, and I was on my bike. We rolled right past each other. We were so baffled and joyful to see each other again. Parents were okay, after all. They had the power to bring us together again after two years of being apart.

She was the friend that always left the door open. It was never closed to me. I had female cousins, was always surrounded by women and I was less scared of girls than other boys would be. They weren't weird to me. Girls symbolized comfort and safety, especially after I had been sexually abused. I could not understand the aggression that boys possessed. I swore I would never be this way, so where would my place be as a boy?

This type of contemplation, coupled with my parents' separation, created isolation. What does this mean to my developing emotional mind? At that time, it meant that my father didn't love us enough to stay and even though my parents told me it wasn't my fault, what I remember is them fighting every morning about issues that seemed to be about me. I am the youngest of three, being the only boy and the baby by thirteen years. In my young mind, the girls were not to blame. It's just me and my mom and certain expectations start to develop that I don't understand and I'm not even sure my mother is aware they are being set. As a child, I felt a great deal of responsibility to keep my mother happy. What I knew of her work life was that the people she worked for didn't appreciate her as much as she would like and there were even instances when her training of a colleague would lead to them receiving a promotion over her. She was no longer with the man she had fallen in love with, my father, and was now a single parent making all of the decisions. Her home was the one area she felt safe and in control.

Things were never a mess in the house, and I wasn't a problem child by any means. For a while, my experience in being the only child at home was that it was only me—whatever was right or wrong left me as the only person to turn to. I felt as if I had to be the positive constant in my mother's life. She never told me it was her expectation but seeing what she viewed as the things that were "wrong" in her life, I thought I had to be what was "right." This is the most pressure I have ever felt in my entire life, and I was a child. The way I saw it was that she is my mother and I have to not be another problem in her life. With that type of mindset, any faltering is detrimental. My mother seemed to be at her breaking point more times than not and that impacted me as well. Based on how I viewed things, if anything at home wasn't working in a way that kept her happy, I looked at it as my fault, therefore thinking of myself as the problem. If I would upset her it would bring up her unresolved issues with my father, and I felt as if I were a reminder of that disappointing relationship.

I felt that I was the source of my parents' problems and if the source were gone, they would be happier. I want people to be happy, and as a kid, I didn't understand they have to want and be that themselves. I always thought there was something I could do. Keeping my room clean. Being the best student I could be at school. When all those things still did not warrant happiness, in my childlike brain, I was not doing enough. I was still the problem.

Recently, my mom reminded me of a time she was sad over my dad, and I had approached her to see what I could do. She said, "nothing," and I walked away, crying. After asking why I was crying, my answer was, "I thought that when you and Dad got back together, you would be happy." She told me that was a turning point. She realized she was trying to make the marriage work by staying and I was acutely aware it wasn't working. She wasn't happy. To hear her make that statement clarified a lot of things for me. I wanted her to be happy and I would try to do everything I could. And sadly, my next thought: If there is nothing that I can do to make them happy, why am I here?

I remember being in a classroom sitting next to a friend. I actually untied my shoes and tried to strangle myself with the shoelaces. It doesn't get more public and rawer than that.

Sis remembers me calling her, expressing extreme loneliness. I cannot access this memory anywhere. I don't remember calling her. She made it clear that I'm not alone, she loves me, and my being here is not a mistake or problem. That conversation saved my life. I needed to hear one person say to me, "You need to be here," or "I need you here." I didn't believe it myself.

Our friendship has been based on quality and not quantity and has shaped the blueprint for every friendship in my life since her. She'll be my "best woman" when I get married. I was her "man of honor." That is a bond deeper than soil!

There are things that stand out about Sis that made her distinctly empathetic to my situation, even at that age, and able to nurture deep and diverse relationships ever since the shoelace incident. In her words: "I call myself a walking anomaly. I was born to a white teenage mom, who was heavily into drugs. My dad was black. My grandma suffers from severe mental illness, so she kicked us out because I was biracial. We've since healed, love my grandma. She's just really sick. Because of that, it caused me to move twelve times before I was ten years old because we couldn't make ends meet, or Mom was trying to go to school, or she had to take care of her siblings. She was the oldest of five. I couldn't handwrite correctly until sixth grade. I had a survivor mentality and by nature, I'm wired to be a protector. Fiercely independent because I've always had to be. My stepdad had severe bipolar, so we dealt with a lot of that. I had to take care of my sister because of him going off the rails. Being around mental illness my whole life, people depressed or suicidal was not abnormal to me. Going on that journey with Antuan was not abnormal to me."

Sis's life trajectory would be one of magic. She married her high school sweetheart. She earned a doctorate. She's the first female high school principal in the district's history and the first person of color in the district's history. She started out in special ed and she's the principal of an alternative high school. With the community, she has always been welcomed with open arms, and has forged significant connections on boards, paving the way for her to lead anti-poverty and anti-trafficking initiatives. As she says, she "looks after the vulnerable, her calling." And let me just say that they are in damned good hands. That's why I trust her to advise me on what kids of today may need from me and how I can give back.

"They are going to be who they are, and they need us to be there when they figure it out. They are so adamant about living their truth at such a young age, it's refreshing. They need to know people will love them through whatever that truth is. For example, although you are a survivor of sexual abuse, that is part of your story. It's not a label or his identity. So many youths today are going through the same things at hyper speed and louder because you can't hide in the era of social media, and they don't know how to navigate that. I tell my students all the time, you were raised in a generation where all communication is based on a response platform—not connection. It's not a connector anymore. It's a response platform. Kids need to know how to authentically connect, have conversations, work through conflict with someone who is not behind a keyboard. It's okay to have tough stuff. It's okay to have easy stuff if that is your life. You don't have to try to make your life look like someone else's. I tell my students to write their own story."

The position she held for me in that call after trying to kill myself with a shoelace has been a throughline in the kind of person I want to be in my life. I want people to know if you need someone to talk to, or there's something you can't do by yourself, and you don't have anyone else, please let me know. *I am that person.*

CHAPTER 3

Disassembled

*"If you can, help others; if you cannot do
that, at least do not harm them."*

—DALAI LAMA

UNTIL THE AGE of thirty in the safe arms of therapy, I thought the reason I froze when I was being abused was because I was a coward and not strong enough to protect myself. I didn't see that as a viable form of protection. That was a conversation in my mind for years and years. "You're small and weak." "Skinny" is not a means of strength. I think of people who can't lose or can't gain weight. It's not great on either side of the spectrum.

Getting avidly involved in martial arts was the first time in my childhood that I started to appreciate my longer, lean body type. I conditioned into that from training and discipline. My instructor, Tony Parks, was in his early to mid-twenties and saw my flexibility and power. There are two disciplines in Taekwondo: *forms* and *sparring*. Forms are based on timing, flexibility, and power. Sparring, which is physically competing and wearing chest, rib, arm, head and leg gear took me more time to get interested in because it involves fighting. I didn't want to hurt anybody…or get hurt!

I started at the age of twelve. It impacted me embracing the body type I had.

Along my life as a performer, I have come to intimately know that some people really have negative imprints early on about the bodies they live in. The negative self-talk, self-hatred, is absolutely corrosive. I know firsthand, and thankfully, I got over at least that aspect of destructive thinking directly as a result of Taekwondo. But that doesn't mean I was completely self-assured and in love with myself. Quite the opposite. We are made of many physical, emotional, spiritual and mental layers, after all. There are a lot of tests. Some more drastic than others.

By the time that Mr. S entered our home, my sisters were long gone. The agreement that Mom signed with the owner of the house was that if there was anything that needed to be fixed, she would call Mr. S, set up a time for him to stop by the house and then he'd take care of the issue. It was the summer of 1994, and I was home each day. Every morning, I'd wake up, eat breakfast and then call Sis so we could talk through the antics of *The Price Is Right* from our separate houses. Other summer favorites were *Supermarket Sweep* and *American Gladiators*. We'd talk about how we wished there were kid versions for each of those shows so we could appear on them together and win prizes.

On no particularly special day, Mr. S was coming by the house to look at something that needed to be fixed. He'd get there, I'd let him in, tell him what the issue was and leave him to do his work. If he was able to fix it that day, he would; if not, he'd tell me what would be needed for it, go get the part and then return that same day or another day. If the fixes were simple, or something that might require a minor repair sooner than later, he'd show me how to do it and then I'd share that with my mom. He'd been to the house so many times and looked like such a nice, old man that I never thought he'd be a threat to me.

No one told me that a threat can be a chameleon. No one told me it could be people that you know. No one told me it could be a white man in what you think is his sixties, with glasses, silver/white hair, with a slender frame.

It seemed like any other summer day. I woke up, ate breakfast and started watching TV. Mr. S was scheduled to come by the house to look at or fix something. Once he arrived, I let him in and then went back to the living room while he got to work. After going to his truck, he returned to tell me he was done and that he had something for me. He handed me a small plastic grocery bag wrapped around a brown paper bag with something in it. Inside: a VHS porn tape. He left and I went back to the living room. It was the first video I'd ever been in possession of. My dad had *Playboy* magazines and I'd looked through them before, but I'd never had a video. I was only fourteen and not old enough to get one.

Over the next several days, I watched the tape. There were two TVs in our house, one in the living room, where my mom watched TV and another in a small bedroom that had been converted to my own personal TV room. I was able to hide the video there because I knew my mom would never watch that TV. The next time Mr. S came to the house, I asked if he could bring me another one. He said "yes." I gave him the original and waited for the new one. This became a system in which I'd ask for a new tape and he'd get it. Most times, he wouldn't even have work to do on the house. He would come by for the sole purpose of delivering me a tape. I felt important. Not intimate but powerful in a twisted way.

As I watched more videos, I started to realize that only the men in them were exciting to me, so I asked for videos with only men. With that signature request made, things started to change with Mr. S. In the beginning, he would give me the video and then leave. Now, as I was watching the video, he stood off to the side to watch me. I didn't want to acknowledge him, so I focused on the TV. Over time, he moved closer and closer to me until one day, he knelt next to me, asking if he could touch my leg.

Looking back at that time, I was so confused. I was fourteen, my hormones were amped up and I had access to videos that I didn't know how to get from anyone else. I didn't have any close male friends, and even if

I did, I wouldn't have been able to tell them that I liked watching guys have sex. I also didn't know what would happen if I rejected Mr. S. Would he stop bringing me the videos, or even worse, would he tell my mom about them? Not seeing any other way out of the situation, I gave him permission to touch my leg. I wish that I could say that would be the only contact he would ever make, but I can't. I don't know if I'll ever be able to forget how dry and rough his hands were, or the way he smelled of dust and oil. Or even the way his body reacted as he got excited.

The most confusing part of all of this for me was how my own body responded to what he was doing. In my mind, I didn't want him to touch me at all. The sight and smell of him repulsed me. Yet, my body was the opposite. Just as I did when I was eight and under the weight of my cousins, I left my body. I put all of my attention into the TV, making it my safe haven. I would feel guilt and shame about what was happening, and I would even blame myself for it. I believed that since I started asking him to bring me gay porn, it made me a willing participant.

Over time, I began to learn that I could control him. I could tell him when and if he could touch me. It was the only way to have any kind of control in the situation. Unfortunately, that would become the foundation for so many relationships I'd have with men in the future. This experience would solidify how to be disconnected, guarded and manipulative. I know that molesters are ruthless and mentally ill to begin with, but that was bold of a handyman to freely drop off porn tapes—blatant physical evidence! We lived in that house from my jr. high years until I graduated from high school. He had all that time to get a sense of who I was, and I have no idea if there were other targets. I was likely not the first. I would ask him questions about what he was fixing. I was a kid with short shorts and no T-shirt on. He said something to the fact of "looking so strong," something that would be gratifying to me about my physicality. I cared about how I looked and enjoyed hearing those things. As experienced predators do, he lured me in, and I bought into it.

I spent four years in Taekwondo trying to make myself believe I was strong and then at the tail end, this happened with the maintenance man. All the training was rendered completely useless. I know now it wasn't because I was at fault, weak or "asked" for something else to happen to me. It just spoke to the craft of a sexual predator. I want to highlight here the way in which I learned to survive and cope with his abuse would directly impact the way I treated any man I was in a physical or emotional relationship with. The way I learned to manipulate the maintenance man was how I felt safe. *I'm going to tell you when you can touch me. I'm going to tell you what videos to bring me.*

I watched one of the porn tapes in the living room and absent-mindedly left it in the VCR. My mom came back home from work for something, and she needed the VCR and found a tape in it. I had taken a speed writing course in high school and ripped the labels off the tapes and wrote the names in speed writing. She watched the tape, not knowing what was on it and called me to come home from school. "What is this? Where did you get it?"

I said, "Mr. S," and she asked me if I liked what I saw. She was livid. But she also had to get back to work.

Needless to say, Mom called our landlord and told them about it, but apparently, even with this disturbing information and my mom's wrath, they acted like they couldn't find another maintenance person. They had used him for years. I thought my mom was going to kill the man. Her personality changed. She grew overprotective the next few years. Who could blame her?

I couldn't admit that I liked the movie or that would have brought up another nest of questions that I wasn't ready to answer. I'm not sure how specific I got. I went back to school that day, which seems remarkable and absurd. Mr. S must have been in his fifties, early sixties at the time. He had a very specific smell of sweat, dust and oil. Over the years, the combination of those smells would come across and a shudder in my body would occur. I would immediately think of him and those dry hands.

We have all been damaged by others. Me, my sisters and my mother, though they didn't talk much about it. I can't help but wonder if I would have spoken up much sooner had I known what had happened to them. There were very few examples of healthy communication. I had truckloads of examples of unhealthy communication. My training was more along the lines of, *this doesn't feel right to me so let me try to figure out what is opposite!* That's almost impossible to do as a child.

CHAPTER 4

Bright Lights, Small Town

AFTER THESE DISTRESSING experiences, my best strategy was to earn good grades and push myself in school rather than retreat into other layers of weakness that I thought I had. Inside, it felt like standing on the edge of a cliff with an abyss underneath.

As a freshman, I tried out for a school play. Even though the role was not a speaking part, I took that "little role" (my mother's words) as chauffeur with a black cap and boots on and stood out.

Kittie Harden was my high school theatre teacher that introduced me to musical theatre. She was the first teacher to see my talent and nurture it. She did more for me than teach. She became a mentor and confidante. I'm her unofficially adopted third son and have stayed in touch with her since I graduated high school in 1998.

She chose me to sing in the chorus of *Annie*, calling my performance "wonderful." That stuck. I wanted to be wonderful in many more roles.

When the department held auditions for *Hello Dolly*, Kittie planned to make it a big dance showcase with an amazing choreographer. I didn't show up to the audition. As part of the audition, students had to sing a prepared song and having not prepared a song, I didn't sign up to audition. Well, Kittie wasn't having it. She sent her assistant, Allison, to track me down with a big audition packet. This teacher believed in me, so I didn't want to let her down. I auditioned and sure enough, landed a spot as one of the principal dancers.

In her words: "Antuan had never had a dance lesson before the show his freshman year, but he was the best dancer. As he started growing into it and realizing what he could do, me and others tried to encourage him. I would say, go, do it! He was a natural. Some people have that 'it' factor, and I've had a handful of students that have it. He was one of mine. We had several amazing students come out of that program. He was one who stood out. It came easy. He didn't take advantage of the fact it came easy to him. He worked hard. He always had things ready before they were due. He was that prepared."

The following year, with her fiery encouragement, I was a featured dancer in *Guys and Dolls*. I remember doing big toe touches and traveling around the stage. That kind of big, wide movement with my body made me feel powerful and strong.

I craved more and more opportunities.

When I was in the children's ensemble, an unpaid position, for *Joseph and the Amazing Technicolor Dreamcoat* at Starlight Theatre, the music director, Molly Jessup, came up to me after a rehearsal and said that she was so impressed with my professionalism that she wanted me to audition for *School House Rocks Live!* at the Coterie Children's Theatre in Kansas City. I was sixteen, so she would need to talk to my mother about me auditioning. I'd show up to the audition expecting to see other high school students, and to my surprise and slight terror, I was the only one, as everyone else was twenty-one and older. Somehow, I stayed, even though I was filled with the fear and insecurities of being a high school student in a room full of adults. I'm so glad I didn't leave because that audition is among the most fun ones I've ever had. We played a lot of improv games, making it feel more like recess than an audition. I left the audition beaming, excited to tell my mom about the experience. By the time I got home, the company had called to offer me the lead of "Willis." I couldn't believe it. It was my first lead role in a musical and at a professional theatre.

When I think of Kittie Harden's early influence on me, I remember her words, "The worst thing is not showing up. I can't cast you if you don't audition."

I walk through numerous doors to show up, never knowing and sometimes not caring what the outcome will be before me. She also taught me to respect fellow actors. She produces a fine arts academy in the summer with high school students and has selected me to be a guest speaker several times. I've talked about professional colleagues going out to party and not being able to perform for matinees. The excellence that I expect in others is definitely what I expect of myself.

Kittie herself is a beacon of excellence and a big advocate for the arts.

She explains, "All kids would benefit greatly from being in theatre. What we all get from being involved in theatre is empathy through playing a character. High school and college students think the world revolves around them. Theatre gets them outside of themselves. Learning from great literature is such an amazing way to grow. Students today are consumers, but they need to be producers. It doesn't do anyone good if all they do is consume. They don't do anything with the information and gifts they have if they just consume it and never share it. No one benefits from that. Theatre allows you to give that gift to an audience and it's all about giving a gift to the audience. We work a long time to put this gift together for our audience. I try to encourage them to think of it that way. It's not about you. It's about what you can give."

CHAPTER 5

Hitting the Books and Boys

"Deceiving others. That is what the world calls a romance."
—OSCAR WILDE

GOING INTO COLLEGE, I was very curious about other guys, but I had scar tissue from what had happened so I made a promise to myself that I would not allow another male to wield control of my body. That meant sexually speaking. To be blunt, I would only be the penetrator. I would only top. Any attempt for that dynamic to shift, my guard would go up even higher and stronger. It became very important for me to maintain that dynamic, whether in a relationship or sexual encounter. I also learned by Mr. S how to be manipulative. I thought other males would look at my frame lustfully and assume I would be submissive. I had to figure out ways to assert myself. That resorted to flirtation, finding ways to emotionally disarm them. I didn't have a checklist. I just figured out tactics based on who the men were. I became a stellar people reader. There were a handful of instances during college where I would meet someone and something about them intrigued me enough that I was willing to reverse those dynamics or allow them to be reversed. Those were very few occurrences.

I didn't believe I could be "in love" with a man. Within the raw experiences with my cousins and Mr. S, after all, love was not in the equation. Nothing I had been taught or told in church or socially led me to believe otherwise. "Homosexuals are deviants." "They are perverts." There was never a conversation around same-sex couples loving and caring about each other. In that absence of knowing, I set out to use men as sex objects and not care about the outcome. Feelings were so damned overrated anyway.

I was eighteen years old when I met a gorgeous, fair-skinned guy at a club. He had his own apartment, and we dated my entire freshman year, yet I never called him my "boyfriend." We had sex in the manner I wanted, which made me feel in control. The first time he told me he loved me, I felt sheer terror. I was not sure I fully believed him. I didn't have a reference point to have these words as a reality. Flesh was reality. Flirtation was a means to the flesh. When I went to college, I thought I could explore freely, no emotional attachment, and then at some point, I would find a woman and get married. I honestly thought that would be my life.

With the radio on, muffling my words, my response was, "thank you" to this man who said he loved me. I felt small and uneventful in my response. But that was the emotional life I was creating for myself. I could have a great life doing other things out of love—namely dancing, and I could love friends and family.

From ages eighteen to thirty, at some point in every relationship, I would think to myself, *what could go wrong with this if I admit I love this person? If someone said they loved me, what are they really trying to get from me?* Love came with ulterior motives. *If I say this to you, I want something from you.*

I had several layers internally that prevented love from entering. They could say it until they were blue in the face, and I didn't believe I was worth loving. My thought was, *you don't know how much I hold from you emotionally.* Cooking dinner, dining out, doing all these things is still not an expression of love. It could end tomorrow, and I will not be hurt or sad. I had a wall up inside. I was very convincing, but in ways obviously, a cold partner but a good manipulator. My actions were not as genuine as they could have been. They were crafted and created from a place of fear in order for me to feel the most empowered of the two of us and be safe. Let me tell you, there are consequences to not letting anyone in emotionally. You can busy yourself and compartmentalize your emotional life, but sexual orientation is not going anywhere. Your emotional palette is not going anywhere. That is why we have hearts! Unless we are among the sociopathic population, emotions catch up. I felt like an asshole inside. I still wanted to be with someone very much.

I met Neil Totton, my brother from another mother, within the first two weeks of college. He was the first gay black man I'd seen that was my age and unapologetically himself. Neil, whom I now call my "sister-brother," used to call me "girl" in college, which pushed every button of insecurity I had as a gay man! This wasn't his intent. It was a term of affection. He knew I was struggling, split in two.

CHAPTER 6

A Sinful Love

*"All great artists draw from the same resource: the human heart,
which tells us that we are all more alike than we are unalike."*
—MAYA ANGELOU

ONCE I KNEW I could have emotional feelings for a man, there was no way I would be with a woman. I had to admit to myself that I didn't have an actual sexual attraction to women. Okay, so no love for men and no desire for women. Would that make me asexual my entire life? That didn't feel congruent either.

Cupid must have been tired of my antics because I would meet Donnie. He is the first man I would love and would also be my first true heartbreak. There were two gay bars in my college town. One that Neil and I frequented called Martha's Vineyard and another for men over forty. One night, I saw this guy dancing, *sooooo* cute. We noticed each other and talked a little bit.

For months thereafter, I would have a recurring dream of this dancing silhouette. I went back to Martha's Vineyard and to my surprise, saw Donnie again. He was the silhouette I had been seeing for months. I thought, *I am not leaving this bar without his phone number.* I was twenty or twenty-one and we started talking on the phone a lot because he lived forty minutes from my college, and he worked as a truck driver. After weeks of phone conversations, we scheduled a time to meet during the winter. Our visit would be postponed after the pipes in his apartment burst. Once we started spending time together, I couldn't see him enough. I remember going home from college one weekend, listening to Christina Aguilera's song, "What a Girl Wants," and rewriting the lyrics, changing the pronouns. It was how I felt about Donnie: IN LOVE. It was my love letter to him.

We planned to spend Valentine's Day together and he cooked me stuffed mushrooms for dinner, which I'd never eaten before. They were delectable. At this point, I'd written another love letter, expressing everything in clear terms that I had never expressed to any other guy. That night, we had sex for the first time, and I bottomed for him, which was a huge deal for me. Later, sitting in his living room, he told me that it wasn't working. *Not working*. That meant that we weren't in love? I was in complete shock. I grabbed my stuff and left Donnie's apartment immediately. No discussion. It was late and raining hard. I cried harder. At midnight, I called Sis. I felt like a fool because I had exposed myself in such a deep emotional and physical way, things I had never done before, and received this horrible outcome—reaffirming all the fears I had. It stiffened my resolve. *This is why you don't express yourself or offer yourself up!* I doubled down on the thick armor I had in place for so long. I could pour every ounce of love into building my dance career and would be just fine.

CHAPTER 7

Dancing on the Water

*"The biggest adventure you can take is to
live the life of your dreams."*

—OPRAH WINFREY

WHEN I WAS a child, younger than ten years old, we lived in an apartment complex that had a pool, and a teenager tried to drown me at a barbeque. I had accidentally poked him in the eye and later that day, we were in the shallow end of the pool. He acted like he was going to help me out but pushed me down. *Down. Down.* Until I couldn't breathe. I'll never forget that horrible experience of almost drowning.

It's a wonder that at the age of twenty, I would audition to perform on a cruise ship for months on end. But remember my comment about walking through doors and being open to the outcome? Even when there is fear. Even when there is the unknown, sometimes the answer is to show up. Low and behold, I got the job, which would lead to a life at sea for two years.

On every cruise ship, you have safety training for logistics. I acquired another type of safety training. I learned to be okay being by myself. I was twenty-three when I started working on cruise ships and until my first cruise ship, I thought I constantly needed to be around people. Then I figured out I was an introvert.

I once did a whole year on a ship for Holland America. Our contract was a world cruise, 108 days starting in California and making our way around the world back to New York. After six months, you have the option of staying on. Six out of eight of us made a pact together to stay, including my dear friend, Melissa Gabriel. It would be easier to adjust to two new people rather than a whole cast.

Talk about overcoming fear or turning it into your fortune. Melissa was not afraid of water. She was afraid of the first show we'd learn, and arguably had good reasons, and I am inspired by her resilience. A resilience that has allowed for her and her husband to have spent the last seven years performing on cruise ships around Australia. Melissa is from Shreveport, Louisiana. My third contract on a ship was her first. The first week, she almost quit. Everyone else had done the show we were learning already. She was spiraling and we had an intervention to save her from jumping ship.

In her words: "I've been performing since I was six. I worked at Disney, Universal Studios. I could learn shows, but the process, I had no idea. I was twenty-five and could do quick pace. You do a lot of shows during the 365 days of a year. When I left Orlando and arrived in LA, Antuan and I lived together. My saving grace was that our company manager and dance captain were a married couple. They negotiated their own living arrangements, and my lead male vocalist had a fiancée in our orchestra, and he chose to do his own living arrangement at a hotel. The female lead vocalist's husband was the golf pro on board from Australia, so she lived in the apartment for two or three weeks only because they got their own space. Other dancers lived at home with their parents. Antuan had a bedroom to himself, and I had an entire bedroom by myself. We had a two-bedroom, which is rare in any sort of cast.

"The itinerary we had was unheard of. Everyone else had worked together. Antuan had done one or two contracts before. He knew the process. When we met, we clicked and were able to develop our lifestyle together. When rehearsals started, I was a fish out of water though. A cast of eight. We worked six days and were meant to have Sunday off. Monday was a vocal day. You walk in and the vocal coach is there. You sing through every single part. These shows are forty-five or fifty minutes. The first show was *They Write the Songs*. Little did I know, the four singers that had already worked together had already done this show. Antuan had two songs out of maybe forty. Because I was the singer-dancer, I had half. I was more than stressed because everyone knew their harmonies. I had one day to record everything for that one show. I basically had a breakdown. And on and on.

"Antuan is the most patient, kind person. If I had been put in this situation with anyone other than him, I'm not sure what I would have done. He was my cheerleader through it all. I am my worst critic. I was crying myself to sleep, then next day, I would put on a happy face and try to work it out. On the Friday that we had the run-through, my brain was mush. I couldn't remember anything. I had no idea what was happening. I pushed myself as a performer. This was the first time I was questioning my ability for what I had been doing my entire life. My producer had to coax me out of the bathroom. Each week was a different concept to learn. This is not real. Antuan tried to calm me down to no end. I called my mom and dad and said I was coming home! They basically told me to get myself together, that I was capable of this. I took out a notebook and put in every dance step, everything until it could work for me. Antuan coached me through my feelings. I don't think I would have stayed if it weren't him, his spirit and who he is as a person. The first week, people probably thought, *why is she here?* This was what I put in my head, self-sabotaging. A lot of us performers do this."

This all-consuming experience was quite pivotal for Melissa. She swore she would never do ships again after that contract. Well, she found love on the water. She and her husband met in 2008 and moved to Singapore. They opened the Universal Studios there and met a ton of Australians, and so began their Australian life after they auditioned for another cruise ship in 2012.

We always get asked what it's like to perform and live on a ship.

By the guests, you are treated like gold. Staff can be different. The Dutch officers of Holland America only took to the female entertainers, though some were closeted and sleeping with the male entertainers. There was animosity. However, I would never get paid so much to do so little. We learned five shows but would only perform them one night a week. Two dinner sittings, which are less than an hour a piece, with sometimes up to a week and a half of not performing. The rehearsal time before you board the ship is a beast though because you rehearse eight hours a day, six days a week. You're on a ship away from everyone in your life. The crew can be working twelve hours or more a day with staff that is strictly hotel, and another, food and beverage.

In many ways, I may be the first to state that the cruise ship industry is problematic when it comes to labor laws. To put it plainly, a lot of what happens I can't imagine would be legal if we were on land. For hotel staff from Indonesia, they send money home, have wonderful houses, a family, but the downside is the amount of time they work. On the ship, you see the same faces month after month. We would have dressers who set up our stage, managed sets and dressed us backstage. We would also see them working in the restaurant. They would invite me for drinks at 1:00 in the morning, living it up for several hours, and then be up bright and cheerful, saying hello to guests at 6:00 a.m. The captain is in charge of getting us where we need to go. The hotel manager runs it all. They have encountered kids straight out of high school, with access to a lot of alcohol and making a ton of money. All told, this unique set of circumstances can create a provocative tale. Being recognizable as the only Black male performer, I was very aware of conducting myself in a way that would keep me in line and out of trouble...for the most part. I was single and in my twenties, after all.

I grew to find comfort in talking with strangers while working for Holland America. It also allowed me to make friends with people all over the world. During one of my contracts, I was at dinner one evening and sitting next to me were two newlyweds in their mid- to late twenties from Ohio who were enjoying their honeymoon on the ship. Throughout the course of our meal, we started talking and I shared with them that I was a performer on the ship. They had not seen our show with the husband admitting that after seeing the movie version of *Rock of Ages*, he had no interest in seeing a staged production because he was worried it would be the same as the movie and he didn't like the movie at all. After dinner, the three of us and another cast member went to one of the onboard bars for drinks. By this point, I had been in the company of the newlyweds for close to an hour and the husband asked if he could ask me a question.

What he wanted to know was if the male performers were gay. I could tell he was asking out of genuine curiosity. For all he knew, *all* men that are performers are gay. He had admitted to not knowing more than where he grew up in Ohio and I can only imagine by his demeanor that very little of his life experiences had put him in the company of many performers, let alone gay men, so how could he know? I assured him that I take very little offense to anything and that I'm not going to be mad at someone asking a question because they want to know more. My answer to his question was that it varies from cast to cast. I've been in shows where I was the only gay man in the cast and others where there were one or two men that weren't gay. There is no exact science to it.

I commend that passenger for asking the question because he could have hidden behind the fear that I would be offended by it, that he would sound ignorant, or even that his wife would be embarrassed by him asking it. Instead, he took the opportunity and spoke his mind and I appreciated it. Not long after we had that conversation, he asked if I was in a relationship myself and I shared with him that I was. That evening of conversation with this couple is one of the things that I most enjoyed when I worked on ships years ago. It's the opportunity to connect with people from all walks of life. I may not enjoy it all the time, but it's there. I had an opportunity to share myself with two people that see the world much differently than I do and were open to see beyond their view long enough to make a connection with someone else. I see that as a gift, one that is readily available to any one of us, and also one that not everyone would welcome.

CHAPTER 8

Where Dreams Are Born

"Reality is wrong. Dreams are for real."
—Tupac Shakur

I APPRECIATED ALL of my cheerleaders in Missouri, but it was time to leave for the expansive world out there. Time to pursue the city that never sleeps but always dreams. (Thanks, Delta, for the fitting quote.)

I moved to New York in 2006. No time for sightseeing though. I quickly jumped onto the island of Manhattan with tens of thousands of musical theatre talents from around the world to take a bite out of the Big Apple. The difference with me was that I wanted a gigantic bite that would last. Like from the crimson king apple.

I had been auditioning every week for a couple of months, going to five auditions a week, and sometimes two in a day if I could. From those auditions I'd book work from May through September. Once September hit, I didn't have anything for that month, but knew I would start rehearsals for a new job in October. For some reason, I got very anxious about not having work for that one month.

After a few days of anxiety, I had a pep talk with myself to remind me that this would be the longest time I'd ever gone without a performance job since I started working professionally twelve years prior. I had discovered a pattern and that pattern was that when there was a time in my life that work slowed down, it usually meant I was in need of my own recharge.

Whether up or down, it was incredible to have the support of a fellow dancer at home. Neil and I were eighteen years old when we met in college in Missouri. We could chat, laugh over ridiculous TV shows, break down or just bust a move in between running to the next gig, and understand each other. I'm so glad that he was my roomie in New York. I don't think anyone else would do during this phase of our lives. We've always had different temperaments and approaches to materializing what drives us though, which makes for good chemistry...and combustion!

Neil's mother used to take him to aerobics with her. A couple of things made that a special occasion: the instructor was really handsome, and he loved the high-energy music. In the performing arts world, you won't always be the top pick. You have hot moments and dry spells. In his twenties, Neil started getting frustrated with the hotter moments. He landed a job teaching Pilates at Alvin Ailey Extension School. The class became popular, then he realized he could do this at other studios. Word started to spread and then Neil entered in *New York* magazine's top trainer competition. He was selected as one of the top ten trainers. That attention he wanted as a performer found him in the business space.

Over the years, Neil is someone who has blossomed in the sense of understanding what a rewarding spiritual journey could look like. Before he and I left for New York City, he had lived in London for a stint as reactions to 9/11 were rather horrendous and imposing abroad. This gave him a wider cultural lens though and changed him forever. He gave himself permission to not ascribe to what his parents, or a small community in Missouri, believed.

In his words: "I am really ambitious, if not overly ambitious and aggressive. If I want to make something happen, I will burn myself to the ground to make it happen. Antuan is more laid back, he gathers inside observation before he acts on something. When we were younger, I thought he was not motivated enough or 'lacks something' but at the ripe age of forty, I realized I could have had more of that for myself. Sometimes you're not aware of all of the roadblocks and booby traps and delusions that one can be under in the insistence of reaching a destination. Seeing his approach now is very inspiring. It's the analogy of the tortoise and the hare! The slower, steady approach has value. I've been in a perpetual cycle of running fast, getting to a destination that wasn't all that, being tired, burning out, staying in that exhausted state and then rebooting and finding wherewithal to do that all over again."

I don't know about the comparison of "tortoise and hare," but we have certainly balanced each other out over the years. When you embark on the journey of leaving your hometown for a bigger city, let alone New York, the mother of all cities, and have someone to grow together and witness each other's evolution, it's really a life experience like no other.

One major thing that expressive and open New York, with all of its wonderful freaks, gays, and ethnicities, forced me to reconcile with was being black and gay and raised as a Christian. I grew up in the church attending Sunday school, Sunday service, Bible study on Monday, and choir on Wednesday. That was the routine. As a child, I constantly heard "God created Adam and Eve, not Adam and Steve," not fully understanding what it meant or the damage it would later cause me. As I got older, that narrative set in, and those cuts that lay dormant for so many years, began to open. The most painful step I'd take to be my true self was coming out to myself. Me saying, I am gay! I wouldn't fully embrace that until the end of college. And again, in every message I had heard in church about homosexuality, love was never a piece of that conversation. Instead, we were defined as *molesters. Sex addicts. Fetishists.* My church didn't talk about love and trust in regard to the LGBTQIA+ community; those were gifts to only be bestowed to heterosexuals. For much of my twenties, it was all about satisfying my sexual needs, not realizing the other hot-blooded, warm-fleshed being was looking for someone to love, someone to satisfy their emotional needs. I had to take a good look at the frame of my life and decide what the picture would be. I dated two different girls in high school and the reason I didn't have sex with them was that I was terrified to become a teenage father. It only takes one time! Whatever the girls were comfortable with, I did, and they weren't in a rush to have sex, fortunately.

I thought my attraction to boys came from a sense of belonging. I finally found boys in theatre and choir, who shared the same type of interests. It was a connector for the jocks and nerds. They played football, basketball, baseball, and they were singing with me. I thought my attraction was mere mutual interest. Looking back, I was physically attracted to them as well. Religion became my greatest strength as I navigated my sexuality, and as with so many LGBTQIA+ people, it can be the source of our greatest pain. My mother is very religious, and in college, I came out to her three times. *Three times!* The issue came from how I phrased it, stating that I *thought* I was attracted to men, coupled with her follow-up questions that I was not prepared to answer. She flat-out asked me if I had sex with men. I was not ready to talk about that. Therefore, she thought it was all in my mind. There was no life to my statement.

Years later, in New York, where other men weren't sleeping, I met someone after a few months of living there. I was excited about living in this incredible city and meeting someone. Early into our relationship I'd be offered a job as a dancer for *Radio City*, a job that would take me out of New York for two months. Four days after I got the job, Jason said, "What does that mean for us?"

My answer was simple: "Let's talk on the phone every day. I still want to hear about your day."

We both decided to move forward as a couple, knowing we'd be apart. I knew it was risky territory for rejection, but I was so elated that I called my mother and somewhat shouted, "Hey Mom, I met someone, and his name is Jason!" She went into theatrics. No, I mean it. I could hear her turn on her breathing machine, having had asthma for years, acting like I threw her into an attack on her physical body. Well, that closed the door to further conversation on my part, but she still sent me *Bible* scriptures to read. The more she sent, the more it confirmed to me she didn't see me as her son, but as some sort of unforgivable sin. If I read those scriptures, I would just be giving into her pain, so I didn't read them for the longest time.

When we met, Jason's parents were Baptist missionaries in South Africa. He grew up having to memorize the *Bible*. Believe me when I say that I could not have been in a more supportive relationship at that time of my life. He even provided me with scripture that would contrast her beliefs. How lucky is that? I honestly loved him for his compassion and unique understanding of my needs. He didn't press me to respond to my mother in one way or another, but he wanted to see our reconciliation and my happiness.

I asked Jason what stood out about our time together, memories and what he may have learned from me. Truth be told, I thought I might get a laugh, too.

He graciously offered in an interview with my collaborator, "That Antuan respects his body and is always prepared whether he needs to be or not. That is a strong trait. His dedication. He doesn't look down on different facets of the work. The work is the work. He stays humble and takes the gig he can get. There is even a video of him dancing in the window of a Marc Jacobs dressed as a pig. He does the work. He gives everything what it deserves. He brings a lot of play to what he does. He is very playful. When he was performing at *Radio City* for Christmas, he would watch from the sidelines and learn the choreography and play with it. When a choreographer stops a performance to make it look cleaner, edgier, with that show especially, they cleaned it with such precision, it's like they clean it with battery acid, it's so tight. That inspires him and challenges him. The fact that he is playful and entertained by the work as well, makes him a better performer. Everything he does is a springboard for something bigger or more important. He also loves him some TV. He can watch the hell out of TV! He has a big, boisterous laugh. It goes back to his diligence and doing the work. I remember visiting him while he was working out of town and finding bags and bags of frozen peas in the freezer, and he doesn't eat peas. They were for his muscles, his legs while he watched television to decompress. Especially when he was in *Radio City* and he had to be the Russian bear!"

There was a lot of scar tissue to heal between my mother and me. The biggest wound would come after I unknowingly made her feel as if she wasn't being heard. She shouted, "It's because of my prayers that God hasn't struck you dead!" Wow. What? How did this happen? Are these really the thoughts of my mother? And could my existence in this world have nothing to do with the good human being that I am?

A year passed before I brought this episode up. She said that she expressed that only because she was upset. I urged her to choose her words more carefully, even more so when she's upset because there is power in words. What you say matters. You can say it. You also have to own it.

As I processed this, I realized that it was because of my faith that I could process it. If I had heard those words before my own spiritual reckoning, I would have been in a much darker place. I understand how LGBTQIA+ people in the closet have committed suicide. If your family that you are connected to by blood and life uses words of harm, or death toward you because of who you are innately, why would you believe that other people will give a damn about you? Who is giving you hope? It can be even more damaging the younger you are because your world is smaller.

Sadly, Jason and I would break up, and it's because he was hungry for a relationship that had growth and goals attached. For him, I froze when it came to homing in on the future, living together, and other things like marriage. He needed to know what we were growing towards. We weren't moving in the same direction Jason imagined himself going. It was never a matter of not loving me; we just had to redefine who we were to each other. We could be better friends than we ever were as boyfriends.

In 2008, with that breakup and "God showing me the way," I was in a form of depression for some time. My mother called and queried, "What is wrong with you? You need to feel better!" But it had been better. I was dating and feeling emotions.

I asked her, "Will you ever want to know anything about the man I'm dating?" Her answer was no, which I knew it would be, and my heart broke into jagged edges. I knew I would have to find a way to be happy and I knew it would require me to have distance from her emotionally. I was living in Harlem at the time, so I walked to Central Park listening to the gospel duo, Mary Mary, and wandered through the park about fifty solid blocks, from 110th Street to Midtown, sobbing. I was in mourning and didn't know when we would heal from this. I needed to live the life I wanted to. I knew this. I was prepared for one of us to leave this earth without her ever asking about my significant other. If she told me this was her truth, I had to believe it. My hope would not change who she is.

My faith gave me the strength to keep searching for who I was within my sexuality. I came to this distinction in college when it wasn't expected of me to attend church three days a week. It was up to me to decide what my life looked like from day to day. What do I believe in? Who was I truly designed to be? Was it finite in a set of beliefs written in a book, a building, or more expansive? If my identity was based solely on the restrictions taught by my religion, the one I inherited, I would probably still be in the closet or dead.

With these questions as my guide, I felt free to explore different modalities for the answers. A friend was going to Landmark Worldwide, which offered personal and professional growth programs, and she invited some individuals, which is part of the system. If someone approaches me to share something intentionally, I will trust my gut and go. I don't ask a lot of questions. I was unemployed, with no savings, and paid for each program with a credit card. There were three separate courses that took most people from three to six months to complete. I did it in half the time. Something in me said, *say yes*. In one exercise, we had to close our eyes and think about our biggest fear. As I struggled to pinpoint my own, I started to hear people giggling. What is so funny? I didn't get it that night, but it would come to me later in a very unexpected way. Days later, while wearing wooden-soled cowboy boots and listening to music, I found myself a few feet behind two Black guys walking in the same direction. Somehow, I startled one of the guys enough that he stopped and asked what the hell I was doing. I'd scared the shit out of *him*.

Once I got inside my apartment, I laughed. I had scared another Black man, but that was my biggest fear—that I would be in spaces with other Black men, and I would be their target. It all led back to the sexual abuse inflicted on me by my male cousins. That experience had imprinted in me how unsafe other Black boys and men could be. Other attempts of bullying in high school, which I now recognize as posturing, by other Black boys, also led me to feeling unsafe and defensive when in the company of other Black males. I realized that *we all feel threatened!* Much of that comes from micro-aggressions. We are all taught to come from a place of fear. When I thought about others feeling this fear, it changed a lot for me. Why the fuck was I so scared? I could move differently in the world now. I wasn't moving in a small way, but it was permission to keep my chin up and see people as human beings, not as a threat or anything negative. That is how I started moving through life, more confident and curious rather than suspicious and fearful.

Secondly, I realized I only believed that any strength I had existed while on a stage and as soon as I left that stage, it was gone. The truth was that strength exists in me as a person. I may access it more to perform, but I don't have to be a smaller person when the curtain goes down and the spotlight goes off. This was a huge turning point.

The same went for my time in Taekwondo as a youth. My strength wasn't a result, it was a display of what I already had.

In the final course of Landmark, we had to create a community project. Part of the success depended on passing the project on so it would exist without you. In the neighborhood I lived in in Harlem, there was a tall iron fence shielding an empty lot with no apartments.

People would walk their dogs and it was a shit minefield, like a lot of places in New York. It annoyed the hell out of me, so I set out to figure out how to provide doggie bags to dog walkers. The solution would be attaching some kind of dispensary box to the fence. I made calls to security in the neighborhood and a PetSmart. I had contacts that would give me bags, but I never got a call back from the building. I had lived in that neighborhood for four years and even though I didn't know my neighbors well, I wanted to contribute to the collective.

Breaking this community initiative down in steps allowed me to come up with a solution. It impacted my life in subsequent actions like writing this book and creating my website.

In a grand finale with Landmark, an exercise was to talk to someone about feelings around an incident that may "help" the other person. Selfishly, I was doing it to get something off my chest. I informed Jason that I had cheated on him several months into our relationship while doing a show. I was misguided in thinking that in doing so, this was necessary for our friendship, a service to him. I burdened him with a truth he didn't need to be burdened with. He was really shocked and sad. He questioned why the hell I would tell him something like this when our breakup was still raw to him. He has such a wonderful heart and spirit and has been a quintessential guide for healing and forgiveness. This last statement shows exactly that. "There are many times Antuan has been a calming factor in my life. Without getting too personal or deep unless he wants to, I don't think anyone understands me like he does or has hurt me like he has or helped heal me like he has. I listen to that Indie Arie song, 'He Heals Me', and I imagine him. Forgiveness is a daily practice. You make conscious decisions in how you forgive and move forward and how you heal."

CHAPTER 9

Stranded in a Show

"I would rather entertain and hope that people learned something than educate people and hope they were entertained."
—WALT DISNEY

NOT ALL SHOWS are long-lasting or groundbreaking. Broadway productions are a different feat altogether. For the most basic explanation of how a theatre is considered a Broadway theatre, I cite *Playbill*, the leading industry reference: "The distinction generally has to do with theatre size (but not 100 percent of the time). Theatres with up to 99 seats generally are considered Off-Off-Broadway; 99-499 seats generally denote Off-Broadway; and 500 and larger generally denote Broadway. There are many exceptions, however, and some overlap. The real key is what sort of contract the production has. The fact that Broadway is the name of a large boulevard in Manhattan sometimes confuses theatre goers as well. Many theatres were located on Broadway, the street, at the turn of the 20th century when the nickname was bestowed. But today, only three "Broadway" theatres are actually on Broadway: Winter Garden, the Marquis, and the eponymous Broadway Theatre. Off-Broadway theatres can be located anywhere in New York, but most are congregated in

Greenwich Village and the West Side. And Off-Off-Broadway theatres are also located throughout the city."

For many, Broadway is the prize for musical theatre professionals worldwide. London's West End is not shabby. It's glittery and prominent for the whole continent of Europe, but Broadway is where I had my sights focused.

As performers though, sometimes we just want to stay in motion when we can't shake it in the bright lights, big city 24/7. We can happily entertain audiences anywhere.

As such, in early 2007, I saw an audition notice for *Jubilee* in Philadelphia. The auditions were on the weekend, which should have been a red flag that the show would not be a quality production. Casting offices work during the week primarily. I went to the audition in some random space, and there were only a couple of other people. A teenager brought over paperwork and asked me if I had music to go with my performance piece. Well, I thought I was going to be taught something and there was nothing in the audition notice that told us to bring prepared material. Lucky for me I had a solo that I'd choreographed while working on a cruise ship a couple of years before.

"So, do you have somewhere I can connect my iPod for music?" The answer was no—red flag number two. I danced and the director was beside himself. "Wow, that was *amazing*! Now, what are you going to sing?" Pause. There was no accompanist. There is an art to holding auditions. It didn't exist on this day.

No surprise, I got called to be in *Jubilee*, but I also got called to be the choreographer!

Thankfully I had the wherewithal to offer to "assist" once we got into rehearsals. The guy who had the idea of doing the show, featuring performers from New York City, had a mentee with him, and the kid started to teach us the choreography. The cast did their best, but patience was the real exercise in performance because the show had no cohesion or professionalism. When it came time to travel to Philadelphia, one of the women said, "I'm sorry, but I'm not doing this."

As the remaining three of us waited to be picked up and taken to Philly, in the heart of winter, a rundown van pulled up. We looked at each other wondering what we were getting ourselves into and then piled in. One of the windows did not close all the way and the row I sat in was a zigzag of ripped stuffing and loose seating that held you in a constant contraction.

We arrived in Philadelphia, two men and a woman, and we were told that a family was hosting us in their house. Our collective response: Hell no! We pulled together and demanded that we be put up in a hotel. We weren't getting paid so it was the least the director could do for us. He was taken aback, but he booked the hotel room. When the other guy and I opened the door to our room, what we saw was one room, one bed! We made it work for one night and then demanded separate beds.

When we got to the community center to rehearse, a tiny space heater was shooting out gushes of hot air, on its last live wire. Okay, maybe it would all burn down, and we would be exempt from performing. Instead, the director kept disappearing into the office upstairs, where it was probably the warmest in the entire building, so we were left to teach the kids all the moves that he was originally supposed to. By the time we did the actual show, the kids were really thrilled and proud of themselves and that was the best part of the entire experience.

Over the next few years, I ran into the other cast members. In fact, the only woman in our cast of misfits was in the audience of *In the Heights* one night and as I walked out of the stage door, we looked at each other, eyes wide. "Jubilee!" That's the worst performance experience I've had, but it was a lesson: listen to your gut and take pride in your level of experience. I had a certain level of professional experience before auditioning for *Jubilee*, and I knew the conditions would be nowhere near what I knew was possible or had worked to achieve.

CHAPTER 10

Heights and Lows

"Fame doesn't fulfill you. It warms you a bit,
but that warmth is temporary."

—Marilyn Monroe

If I had spent every day from the time that I decided to be in this business to the time I joined the magical production of *In the Heights*, making a list of what I hoped my Broadway debut would be and feel like, I still wouldn't have come close to what the reality was. It was that remarkable.

The first time I saw the show before my callback, I was in awe to see this stage full of brown people, which I had never seen before in person. The most modern-day show I knew of was *Dream Girls*. There's three white people in *Dream Girls*. Then to join the cast of *In the Heights* and for so many of us who were then in our mid-twenties to make our Broadway debuts alongside people who were almost fifty making their Broadway debuts, I was in awe. How did these people keep going? They showed me how many opportunities were available to me as a performer offstage as well, like voiceover work and being a teaching artist. I had been so focused on doing this one thing, performing. Yes, I knew people were talking on TV shows, commercials, but I didn't realize it was all connected. Every person I worked with challenged and elevated me as a performer.

My debut on Broadway and all that it signified did not escape my mother thankfully. She will tell you that the deal was whenever I hit Broadway, I would get her to New York. And I did! To the audience, not the stage, but still....

She came to my performance with my youngest nephew, who she pulled out of school to travel with and surprise him. Mom recalls, "I was grinning, then crying, then violently crying because I was looking at my child reaching his goal. I was so happy for him. I don't know about other mothers watching their children perform, but I watched his every move from one side to the other. I didn't watch nobody else, so I'm glad I saw the show again. I had never questioned his talent, but when he left my house, I wanted to be sure he could take care of himself doing this type of work."

Me in action represented to her goals achieved and a steady income, not to mention something to talk about back home in Missouri.

For many performers, a road to getting on Broadway is to travel with a touring company of a show. I was afraid of doing tours because I had only heard of "bus and truck tours," meaning you have a show and then you get on the bus and drive to the next city and do the same thing over and over again. I thought all touring was this, learning later tours existed on many different levels. A first national tour meant you stayed in a city for weeks, even months, and got paid more. That sounded much more interesting! I had already traveled the world on cruise ships as a performer, sharing a cramped space with someone else. I didn't want to do something similar on land. I was twenty-five years old, looking for more opportunities to work and be paid to do what I loved.

In early April of 2010, I had been the vacation swing for the Broadway production of *In the Heights* for almost two years and was in Missouri for a wedding while on vacation. From the wedding, I would be traveling to Springfield, to visit friends and faculty from my alma mater, then head to my hometown of Blue Springs to see more family and friends before flying back to New York. The day before I drove to my hometown, on my way to dinner, I got a call from someone in the production office for *In the Heights* asking if I'd be able to fly to Ft. Lauderdale, Florida in a couple of days to work with the first national tour of the show. I explained that I was currently on vacation and would need to change some things around in order to make it work, but I'd need at least a day to make that happen. They agreed.

In the fever of these decisions, the first person I called was my mom because me flying to Florida meant I wouldn't be visiting her in Missouri anymore and it had been almost two years since I was home. As I informed her of the scenario, feeling sad about not being able to see her, she interrupted with, "You told them you're going, right?" I informed her that I gave them a soft "yes," and that I needed to settle some other plans before I gave them a final answer. I was hoping she'd be a little more upset by me not coming home, but I knew that she had always wanted me to make a living doing what I love and if that meant less time for us to be together, that's what it had to be.

I called the office back to tell them I agreed to their offer, and the next morning, I drove three hours to Blue Springs, having my mom meet me at the car rental place so I could return my car and see her briefly. We got to enjoy an hour of quality time together in the car before I was off on a plane to Florida for what I thought would be a weekend.

I arrived in Ft. Lauderdale with one suitcase and nothing I'd want or need to have to be on tour. I had no clothes for rehearsals and limited toiletries. I made my way to the theatre so I could watch the show that evening in preparation for a possible rehearsal the following day. I'd been working with the Broadway company for almost two years, so there wasn't much that I had to learn from scratch. At the end of that first day, I made a trip to Wal-Mart to buy some T-shirts and athletic shorts to wear during rehearsal, as well as snacks to have in my hotel room. Before the weekend ended, I was called to travel with the tour to the next city of Naples, Florida. Hard stop: This was shaping up to be my life as a swing, just so you can get the picture.

As the week flew by, I was in rehearsal an average of four hours a day, except for days when there were two shows. I fantasized about going back to New York. I was so close. It had been two weeks.

On Friday of that week, I got a phone call from my friend and dance captain for the New York company asking me if the production office had spoken to me about joining the tour for the next six months as an associate dance captain, understudy and swing for the male ensemble. What I didn't know at that time was that towards the beginning of the tour the male dance captain and swing injured himself and was on a medical leave for the show. The production office had found someone from the Broadway company that was able and willing to go out on the tour to fill in for a certain amount of time and now, that time was ending. They would need someone else to fill in. Before we hung up, he urged me to "act surprised" when they brought this up.

I spent the next several hours thinking about if I'd say yes or no. I'd been working with the Broadway show as a vacation swing off and on for almost two years and even though the money wasn't guaranteed week to week, I was home, in New York, and on Broadway! If I said yes to going on tour I'd have to leave, find someone to sublet my room in my apartment, and make all other necessary arrangements. I was over-whelmed, to say the least.

Late Saturday morning, I got the big call. When the offer came after some buttery compliments, I feigned excitement and surprise. They informed me what my salary would be and that they'd like an answer by the end of the day. Did I mention that it was almost Saturday afternoon, and I was under the assumption that I'd be flying back to New York by Monday at the latest and the tour would be moving to its next city that same Monday?

At this point in my career, I had been accepted into the Actor's Equity Union but had no agent or formal representation. (This means that any negotiations that occur happen because I make them happen.) Needless to say, I was very overwhelmed and scared that I would make the wrong decision. After a few minutes, I called Jason for his advice. I explained that my conflict was loving the show so much that I would have done anything that I could for it, but I was also scared to leave New York. I wasn't happy with the money they offered me, particularly because it would mean taking a pay cut from my Broadway salary and I'd have more responsibilities on tour than if I were performing the show in New York.

After a thoughtful pause, Jason advised, "You have the upper hand because they need you to go on tour. You could say no to the tour and the Broadway company would still need you. Also, they know that they are saving time and money by having you go on the tour because they won't have to put in the time it takes to teach someone who is new to the show."

With his consultation, I felt empowered. I thought about what I would need in order for me to say yes to this offer, and I made a list... checked it twice: Broadway salary, return home for a week to get my life in order, and a vacation I'd planned out of the country in a couple of months for two weeks.

I called the office back later that day and offered them my terms with the utmost confidence for the first time in history possibly, and that is why I have gone into this elaborate description. It takes boldfaced courage sometimes to ask for what you want, commensurate with your gifts. My name within the company was "Magic" after all!

After some haggling on their end and a second call, I accepted the offer, and everything was put into motion. I was able to get more money. It wasn't what I wanted, but it was more than they initially offered. I'd fly back to New York to pack up for the next six months of what would be my life on tour, and I set up six interviews for potential sublets for my apartment. Unfortunately, I was not able to find anyone to rent my room, so I left it up to one of my roommates to figure it out, and luck-ily, he knew someone who needed a room. It would be the one and only time I'd have someone sublet my room that I did not meet personally, and let's just say that it wouldn't be a mistake I'd make a second time.

With my bags packed, I made my way to Houston to meet up with the tour. The next couple of months were a blur of rehearsals, watching the show and traveling to new cities. I'd never traveled across the country with a show, so all of this was a new experience. In fact, before this I was very reluctant to do a touring company with a show because as I mentioned earlier, I was horrified at hopping on a "bus and truck tour." The most prestigious tour in the business is known as the "production contract tour." This title is often but not exclusively reserved for the first touring company of a show that is currently running on Broadway. The salaries are higher than most other touring contract salaries, the show will go to larger cities, and it will stay in those cities longer. For example, *In the Heights* spent a minimum of one week in any city we went to and for most of the larger cities like LA and San Francisco, we were there for five weeks. This tour was no bus and truck tour. The only time the cast would travel via bus would be if the travel between one city and the next was at a specific distance that was already outlined in the contract. All travel would be organized by the company manager and before each city, we would be given a list of our hotel options. As per our contract, the actors would receive a weekly tax-free per diem or stipend, which would go towards paying for any housing and meals. We'd get at least two hotel options that would be within a mile of the theatre and then it was up to us to book our rooms. If the hotels were more than a mile from the theatre we would have to be provided with transportation to and from the theatre and that could be rental cars or reimbursement for public transportation. It was also before Uber or Lyft existed. In an effort to save money, many people on tour would split the cost of a hotel room. I wasn't one of those people, at least not very often. I think I shared a room only twice in the six months I was on tour. Having my own space was worth the cost of living alone. After all, I'd spend the majority of my day with the same people, for the next six months and I knew myself well enough to know that I'd want time alone.

I was almost thirty years old, single, ready to mingle and traveling across the country in a hit show! And as love tends to do, it finds you where and when you least expect it. For me, that would be in San Francisco.

Before getting to San Fran with the show, I'd only been to LA and growing up in the Midwest, I thought that *all* of California was warm, all the time. I was very wrong. I arrived in SF with mostly shorts, T-shirts, some jeans, and no jacket. The weather was grey, misty and in the mid-sixties for the first two weeks we were there. I'd been with the tour for just over a month and every week seemed to look like the next. We'd get to a new city and my schedule was that I'd have rehearsal at any available time that didn't include a show happening. If there was an evening show, I'd be in a rehearsal from noon to 4:00 p.m., or 1:00-5:00 p.m., then I'd go have dinner and report back to the theatre in two hours to be on-site for the show, in case I needed to go onstage in case of an emergency. Even when I wasn't in rehearsal, I'd still need to do my own work to make sure that I knew what I needed to know and if that meant getting to the theatre an hour early to walk through the show by myself in order to know where my props were, or to know where a costume change happened, that was what I'd do. It also meant going over choreography in any space I could find in the theatre, and most times, in the hotel room or apartment I was staying in as well as listening to recordings of what I had to sing in the show and making sure that I knew the differences that each man had to sing in the show. With me covering six male ensemble members, as well as understudying a lead, that meant a lot of material to be responsible for.

This is just a portion of the work that goes into the day-to-day of being a swing in musical theatre. This doesn't account for the years, months, days, hours and seconds of training and auditioning spent to capture the job in the first place.

Expecting to be in sunny California with warm weather every day, I was rather disappointed, in addition to having to spend so much time inside. Not having much time or energy for anything that isn't work, my primary source for meeting new people in a new city was online, specifically a website called Adam4Adam, and no, it's not a Christian dating site for gay identifying men, though you can definitely get to know someone in the biblical sense if you're willing to! After scanning several profiles, my eyes fixed on one with a striking photo, so I sent a message. We started to chat and after a few days, I suggested we meet in person. He, whom I'll refer to as "PP," initially agreed but didn't seem anxious for follow-through. I had mentioned to him that I would be leaving within a month. What I didn't know until later was he was nervous to meet me and hoping the clock would run out on my time in San Francisco in the flurry of my activity. Being persistent, I kept trying to meet him and once he learned I was staying longer than he anticipated, we had our first date. I had no expectations about us meeting each other; it could only be for coffee, or it could just be for sex, whatever we both agreed to. What I didn't expect was for him to take me to his favorite places. A drive across the Golden Gate Bridge and up to a lookout point over the bridge, as well as a drive down Lombard Street and a night drive up to the Twin Peaks and Sutro Tower area to see the city lit up and twinkling. It was wildly romantic. It made me feel so comfortable, shattering every negative feeling I'd been having about being on tour and in San Fran.

I had been taken out of my work bubble and placed into reality and it was just what I needed. When you are touring with a show, you are in a different city constantly. You don't get to enjoy the simple routine of cooking your own meals, sleeping in your bed and under your own sheets. You may not have photos of loved ones to look at as you walk around your space and often, you don't even have your own private space because you are sharing a room in order to save money. Sometimes it can be for several weeks or months, or it can only be for the day you are performing. You aren't always able to settle in and feel "at home" so anytime you can capture that feeling in a place that is unfamiliar, is a gift.

For the next two weeks, we spoke to each other daily and saw one another as often as my schedule allowed. Within that time, Neil came in for a visit and would meet PP. One night, after I was done with the show, the three of us met at a diner near my apartment for a late dinner and while we were talking, Neil asked PP "getting to know you" questions. I could tell he was getting nervous by the questions, but I didn't think too much about it.

After a while, PP paused and directed his attention to me. He said that he had been hesitant to tell me that he makes part of his living as a drag queen. My friend quickly replied that I wouldn't care and then I reiterated the same. We talked more about it in private and he explained that it had been his experience that when men found out he performed in drag, there would be one of two responses: complete turnoff or complete fascination, verging on fetishizing it. My reply: "Of anyone you could tell this to, I'm going to understand it. It's what you do to make money, it's not who you are all the time. I work in theatre, but I'm not breaking into song and dance every time I'm walking down the street. I met you as PP and that's who I'm attracted to. Who you are in drag is someone else, as far as I'm concerned, and I can respect that."

I saw him in drag several times after that conversation, and it is a miraculous transformation to witness.

As a kid, I remember being fascinated with watching my mother get ready for work and one time, when she had left the bathroom, I tried to use her eyelash curler and it was a mistake I'd only make once in my life. I didn't know how they worked and almost pulled my eyelashes out of my head. Now, if watching a woman go through that process was fascinating, can you imagine how I'd be seeing a man who's over six feet, who weighed almost 200 pounds transform into his interpretation of a woman? There is skill, precision and imagination involved to make that work, and it's work that I'm not willing to do and can appreciate anyone who does. I was also able to see him as just Her. I knew he was still under the make-up, wigs and padding, but He was a means for Her to exist.

The first time I went to a club where She was hosting, we never talked about what our dynamic would be, and we didn't need to. She was there to work, make money, and entertain and I was there to support. She'd check in with me from time to time, but other than that, I was a guest. It wouldn't be until He removed the make-up, wig and padding that we'd hug and kiss one another as a couple. I can say with confidence that of the many people I thought I'd date in my lifetime, a man who also did drag was not on that list. I learned a lot being included into drag culture. It's a family with mothers, children, and multiple branches of a family tree. They are there to support each other in their lives, both in and out of drag and that can cover topics like sobriety, employment, and relationship advice. The life they live is not as different as the men and women who walk into an office to make a living. What is different is that when they put on their uniforms, they become a target for ignorance and fear. They are a brave and courageous community that is often neglected and ridiculed for what they contribute. Things are definitely different now than they were even ten years ago.

After San Francisco, *In the Heights* traveled to LA for five weeks. PP visited me there and things were going pretty well. A few cities later, I was in San Diego and panicked. I was afraid. Afraid that our relationship didn't make sense because I was on tour with a show and traveling around the country and would be going to Tokyo soon for almost a month. On top of that, once the tour was over, I'd be going back home to New York, and he was in San Francisco. I knew I wasn't going to move, and I wasn't ready to ask him to move to New York. While in Costa Mesa I called him and ended things, expressing all the ways in which our relationship wouldn't work. He did his best to convince me that we could find a way to work it out, but once my mind is made up it's very hard for anyone but me to change it.

A few weeks later, in what felt like a swell of emotion, I called him. I told him how much I missed him and that I knew I had given a list of reasons as to why we wouldn't work, but I wanted us to try. I also shared that I would be leaving for Tokyo in two days, so my timing made no sense at all. Who wants to reunite with someone before they fly out of the country?

At that time in my life, for me, that was my proof that my decision was based on emotion, not a list of what made sense. I had spent most of my adult relationships with men being consciously aware of how much I allowed myself to be vulnerable with them. I seldom said "I love you" first. I never gave them more of me than I was comfortable with, be it emotionally or physically. My facade of confidence, intrigue and interest had been carefully manufactured. But in the moment of being on the phone with PP and spilling my guts out about how I wanted us to Skype every day I was in Tokyo, that facade tumbled to the side. I wanted to follow what I felt in my heart and to my surprise, and delight, he accepted.

We talked to each other every day for the almost four weeks I was in Tokyo, and we were happy. The show would travel to Seattle from Tokyo, and we planned for him to visit me there for a week. That would be my last city with the tour before I went back home to New York. Once I returned home, he visited me, with our next visit together being me going to SF to visit him and then he made another trip to New York to see me after that. This is where it got nerve-wrenching for me again. He started to talk about us being together for Valentine's Day in the upcoming 2011 year. On the inside I felt myself retreat. And not because of memories of the breakup that poisoned my Valentine's Day once before. I just wasn't looking that far ahead. In fact, I hadn't even thought about where either of us would be for the Thanksgiving or Christmas before. He went to the airport, and I already knew that I would not see him again. I did break up with him, with no more reason than the stirring discomfort of someone being able to articulate seeing me in their future, even if it were only several months ahead. Especially when I wasn't sure where I'd be at that time. It was the first time I'd ever had a man articulate any type of future that would include me, and I wasn't emotionally ready to hear that. It felt too big to accept, considering our longest amount of time together had been a few weeks. Looking back at it now, I put a load of pressure on the situation, probably more than it needed. I can now see that I was doing the best I knew to do at that time, both for me and even if misguided, for him.

I can admit that at twenty-nine years old and having turned thirty while we were together, I was selfish. I was selfish about putting my career first and I don't apologize for that. It was the most important thing to me at that time and anyone or anything else would be third on the list at best. I got so much from being with PP and I hope that I was able to give him even an ounce of that in return.

I was, indeed, selfish, but I also pushed physical boundaries that year, which made me grow in other ways. Climbing Mt. Fuji topped the chart!

A large group of eight people were planning to do it on the last full day before we got into the theatre. Once we arrived in Tokyo, we only had two and a half days free before performing. My immediate thought was that they were batshit crazy to climb a mountain the day before our first show, so I declined. There was a smaller group of three, consisting of a fellow swing "D," male ensemble member "O" and our drummer "L," that said they were going to go the day before the larger group and that made more sense to me. At least that way, I'd have a full day to rest my body and if the larger group was going the day after us, I might be performing the show for someone if they didn't come to work.

I joined the smaller group and left all of the planning to someone else. I knew nothing about climbing a mountain and just as much about Mt. Fuji. I didn't know how tall it was or how long it would take us, I was walking in fully naive. The morning that we were to start our adventure, I decided to chronicle the day with video and I'm so glad I did. It took a train and a bus to get us to our starting point, which would be halfway up the mountain. Once we got there, we saw people with walking sticks and collectively decided it would be a good idea to get our own. We learned that you could also get a stamp on them as you passed each checkpoint. "O" had bought headlamps for the group, and we had plenty of water, layers, snacks and towels. We were doing the "sunrise climb," which meant we'd start around 6:00 p.m., get to a rest point where we'd have a hot meal and a place to sleep for a bit. From there, we'd continue to the summit of the mountain with the goal to see the sun rise the next morning. With our walking sticks in hand, we began our journey and passed others coming down from the mountain. Bright-eyed and hopeful, we asked how it went and with almost every person we passed, we heard, "Turn around! Don't do it!" This wasn't exactly the response I expected. I didn't think anyone would be ecstatic about it, but I definitely wasn't prepared for such a strong negative response. At that point, we had paid for everything and I'm not one to waste money, so up this mountain I would stomp!

It was a sunny day with few clouds in the sky and even though it was probably close to ninety degrees in the city, it was in the mid-seventies on the mountain. On our climb, we saw families and groups of all ages and races along the way. We saw a group of at least twenty climbers wearing clown wigs, which was fun. I also saw a family with the youngest being maybe ten years old and the oldest being at what I'll guess was in her sixties and let me tell you that I was very humbled to be climbing the same mountain at thirty years old with a walking stick as assistance. With each checkpoint we'd pay for a stamp to go on our walking sticks and then keep moving. As it got darker, we put on our headlamps and made our way to where we'd be sleeping. When we arrived, there were only a few other people inside of what I can best describe as a room that had shelves built onto the walls. Our hot meal was white rice, curry sauce and pearl onions and having only eaten trail mix for the previous five hours, it was the most delicious meal ever!

We decided to get some rest before we continued up the mountain and then climbed up onto the middle shelf where a thin sleeping bag and a rice pillow awaited us. The pillow was no bigger than what you would get on an airplane. I reminded myself that "comfort" wasn't the goal and settled in for some rest. I think I only napped for about an hour and then one of us noticed that we had become the only people still in the room. It was some time after midnight and with everyone else gone we figured that if we were planning to get to the top before the sun came up, we'd better get moving. We kept climbing, with the temperature a little colder, the sky a lot darker, and everyone climbing in silence. We learned that "D" had asthma and the increased elevation was making his climb more difficult, but he was determined to keep going.

Without warning or even knowing why, my knee started to bother me and each time I had to lift my leg to step up, I felt tightness. I knew that I wouldn't be able to turn around, so I kept going up, being mindful of my knee and using my walking stick more. At this point of the climb, the terrain was a bit rockier and required more stability, patience and awareness.

As we continued, we split off into pairs, with "L" and me ahead of "D" and "O." Eventually I got ahead of "L" and found myself just above the horizon of clouds as the sun started to rise. With less than two hours of sleep, scarce nourishment and a tight knee for over four hours, exhaustion hit. I sat down to see the sun break through the clouds. I had all but resigned myself to thinking that I wouldn't make it to the top of the mountain. I also didn't know how I'd get off the mountain, but that would have to be figured out later. In my exhaustion, I forced myself to be present in the moment. I started to think about my life and the many events that happened before this one. I thought of the challenges I had to overcome to get to this point and I felt thankful. I was somewhere I never thought I'd be, doing something I never thought I'd be doing and in one word, it was beautiful. Even with the pain and exhaustion, it was still beautiful. That's what nature offers us in abundance: beauty. We just have to stop and look beyond ourselves in order to see it.

As I sat taking in the sunrise and watching the colors of the sky change like a kaleidoscope, "L" passed me. She asked if I was okay, and I told her that my knee was bothering me and that I was gonna rest for a bit and then keep going. Sometime after that, "O" caught up to me and asked the same question and then made his way up the mountain. After I'd taken in all of the "moment" (now many minutes) I needed to, I decided I'd have to keep going. I had no idea how far I had to go or how long it would take me, but if my life taught me anything it was that as long as I kept moving, I was going to get somewhere.

I got up and took it one step at a time. In less than fifteen minutes, I found myself approaching a sort of gate signaling I was nearing the summit of the mountain. I was as happy as a kid on Christmas morning. I DID IT, I MADE IT TO THE TOP! I made my way to the line to get my final stamp, having no idea where "L" and "O" were and none of us had any idea where "D" was. He and "O" had separated hours ago. As I stood in line for my stamp, I turned around to see "L" and "O" walking towards me and as soon as we made eye contact, I burst into tears of joy. You see, absentmindedly, none of us thought to discuss what would happen if we were to get separated from each other. We all assumed we'd get to the top at the same time and then make our way to the bottom at the same time. As I sat watching the sunrise and watched them pass me one at a time, I fully expected to not get to the top of that mountain. I thought I might need to be airlifted off of the mountain or at the very least, have someone carry me down. Even though we each had a cell phone, none of us had paid for an international plan. Our only means of communication was verbal. So, to see the two of them walking towards me gave me what I thought would be the greatest sense of relief for that day. We hugged, laughed and eagerly awaited our stamps. We walked around the top of the mountain hoping to see "D" in the crowd, but we didn't. We weren't sure what to do and eventually decided that it would be best to make our way back down, in hopes that "D" would be waiting for us where we all started. The route down was different from the route up and I was so thankful for that. It took all of the pressure off of my knee and put it in my quads and as a dancer, they were well developed and used to working. I think I might be the only person to have enjoyed walking down that mountain, and I understood why every person we passed at the beginning of our climb warned us to turn around.

The path down was on a gravel road that snaked its way through grass. I felt invigorated and refreshed and the most hopeful I'd been in hours. We eventually made it to our starting point and checked the surrounding area for "D" but didn't find him. "L" had plans to meet a college friend for dinner that night and wasn't confident that she'd be able to navigate her way back to the hotel. I insisted that "O" go with her while I'd stay behind and wait for "D." I knew that I couldn't leave without knowing where he was. I positioned myself on the end of a picnic table, with a direct view of the entrance to the mountain. Anyone going up or coming down would have to walk past me. I don't know if I sat there for twenty minutes or an hour, but I know it felt too long. I scanned every face hoping to see his and there were even a few times when a truck would come through and I would look in the back to see if he was in it. The worst-case scenario was that he'd had an asthma attack and had to be carried off the mountain and taken to a hospital. The best-cast scenario was that he was slowly making his way down on his own. Thankfully, the latter was the reality. I saw him, walking by himself with his stick in hand and felt what would actually be the greatest sense of relief for the day. I don't have any children but would compare it to how I imagine it would feel to have lost your child in a shopping mall, to then be reunited with them. We both smiled as we walked toward each other and hugged. He was hungry so we went into a convenience store so he could get something to eat.

My knee still throbbed. I hadn't experienced knee problems before this and was concerned that it would interfere with work. While we were standing in line to check out, I shook my leg to see if I could loosen it up a bit and after a few shakes, I heard a popping sound, followed by a release of pressure. I bent my knee to see if I had my full range of motion and I did. My knee just needed to pop. This day was getting better by the minute!

After getting some food, we made our way to wait for the bus and we saw "L" and "O" still standing in line. They had missed the previous bus and were waiting for the next one to arrive. This moment was such a great representation of the entire experience of climbing Mt. Fuji. What I mean is, we all started the endeavor together the morning before and when fatigue, pain and even asthma separated us, we still found our way back to the group. We each made it to the top of that mountain in our own time and on our own accord while managing to share in that experience together. Even with the pain in my knee I had no expectation that any of them would be responsible for getting me to the top, that was something I'd have to do for myself. And whether I knew it consciously or subconsciously, I knew they would be there for me in some way. We were four strangers, working in the same show together, traveling in a foreign country to all of us, who decided to say yes to the same adventure. Aside from travel, food and lodging details during the climb, we didn't plan much else out in advance and the outcome could have been much different. I can only imagine that it was a sense of respect and care for each other that kept us connected because we sure as hell didn't make a plan for if any of us got separated from the other.

During our bus and train ride back to our hotel we all shared the highlights and lows of the climb and what we planned to do with our evenings. "D" and I went to McDonalds and for what I think might've been the first time in my life, a Big Mac. As a kid, I preferred their nuggets and getting older, I kept my intake from them to anything chicken and fries. Never has a McDonald's burger tasted so good! Especially after not eating a full meal in thirty hours. It could've also been that in Tokyo they use Kobe beef for their burgers. I could taste the seasoning, as if it was made in someone's backyard, on their grill. After eating, "D" and I bought bags of ice. Why ice? I strongly recommended that each of us take an ice bath that night because it helps with inflammation and muscle soreness. I learned that from the years I'd danced in the *Radio City Christmas Spectacular* with the Rockettes. All they'd need to do was to fill a bathtub with cold water, waist deep with a few bags of ice and soak in it for at least ten minutes. It wouldn't be the most comfortable thing, but your body would thank you the next morning. After my ice bath, immediately followed by a hot shower, I got into my hotel bed, fell asleep before 9:00 p.m. and didn't wake up until almost 11:00 the next morning.

That experience is still one of the most challenging and rewarding of my life to date and if I had to do it again, I would. Climbing Mt. Fuji was not something I saw myself wanting to do at any time of my life, let alone even being in Tokyo. I said "yes' on a very ignorant whim with the deciding factor being that I'd have an extra day of rest after doing the climb. I had no expectations and almost as much knowledge. What I did have was a "yes" to something new and a willingness to see where that would take me, and it didn't let me down. I was challenged to a point where I felt uncomfortable and almost defeated and even when I was there, I kept going.

In the Heights asked me for another six months on tour, which I declined. By this time, I wasn't afraid to say no to full-time work. It was my way of keeping a promise I made to myself in college during a production of *Oklahoma*. I was very confident that I would be cast as "Dream Curly," one of two dancing doppelgangers to the dramatic actors who play the same role, with a female dancer who represents the female lead. The dancing trio signifies the love triangle between them. I was the best dancer out of the males in both the musical theatre and dance departments. To my complete surprise, I was not cast in either of the roles. It went to two white men. That was the second time I had this situation. In high school, I auditioned for the lead of *Crazy for You*. I didn't understand the politics of a predominantly white suburban high school or university in Missouri, in the 1990s. Both instances were devastating.

In college, I accepted the role in the chorus of *Oklahoma* because this would be my last show with a good group of friends before they graduated, but I had a nasty attitude. I don't know how nasty I was to anyone else, but I knew how I felt inside, and I knew I had to do something about it. I gathered some of the first-year students and apologized for my attitude—I didn't want to ruin their experience. Because of that experience, I made a promise to myself that I would not be with a show that my heart was not fully committed to, regardless of money or opportunity. I couldn't stomach that feeling again.

After being offered the full-time position of co-dance captain for the tour of *In the Heights* and refusing the position, the other dance captain asked me why I was leaving. I told her I only wanted to be there for six months, as I knew some of the people on the tour wouldn't do well with me as their dance captain because they weren't ready for the type of dance captain I would be. The kind of dance captain who is more concerned with the integrity of the show, not the egos of the performers. I knew enough to not put myself in a position where I could regret going to work each day. With the cast on Broadway, I had seen that even when people were tired or annoyed, once they stepped on stage, they understood the importance of what they were doing for the audience members, especially those of color. What I experienced with the Broadway company was a deep understanding and appreciation for what we were doing. It was the first time in my career that everyone I was onstage with elevated me to be a better performer.

Rickey Tripp, one of the most talented people I've ever known, became a brother to me. He calls me "Twany." (I know, another nickname!) I think he danced out of the womb. No, really! He comes from a family of dancers and for many Black people, dance comes from the community. He went to school to be a pediatrician though and studied biological science for a year. Rickey took a hip-hop class and fell in love. His teacher, who is still a good friend, pressed him, "Try my jazz 2 class next semester."

I love his description of how his shiny dance career took off. "I had no idea what that class would be. She asked me to do a specific movement and I did. She said, 'I thought so.' First day, only guy in the room. I looked a hot mess. I was in class with all these women who had been training the majority of their lives. I know I looked crazy. She started the choreography to Janet Jackson, who I am yet to work with but want to! It's like nirvana opened up. I loved it. As a dance major, in Dance 101, you had to write three essays: concert piece, musical theatre and dance. I saw this company on campus and sitting there, I thought, these people are acting, singing *and* dancing? I have to do this. It was called Company One. I auditioned and the director and I became friends. It changed my life. It was always a part of my life, but I didn't know it was available to me. Coming from the hood, I didn't know you could train for it. I thought it was just for celebrities. But here I am! In 2001, I went to the summer Alvin Ailey program in New York and saw *Aida* from the balcony looking down, and I thought, *that is what I want to do*! I returned to San Jose to graduate in '03. I gave myself a year to figure out commercial dance in LA, videos, commercials, or New York. There was more to me than being a backup dancer. The summer of '04, I worked on a show on the West Coast, then I made it to Broadway."

Rickey's Broadway debut was *In the Heights,* like so many of our tight circle of friends. He then went on to do *Smash* and *Motown on Broadway* before we both found ourselves reunited in *Hamilton.* He even gets to say that he has a part in the movie version of *In the Heights*! Now, as a teacher, choreographer and director, Rickey advises a lot of new blood coming into the city with stars in their eyes. We were both those boys.

"I tell people when they get here, it's important to find your tribe. Now, I'm surrounded by people who allow me to be myself and support me and uplift me. We used to not have job stability. It fluctuates and the biggest challenge is not knowing if your next check is coming. It always works out—I'm very spiritual in that sense. Sometimes you compare yourself to those not in the business and they have a house. *I'm forty-one. What do I have to show for it?* Sometimes the mental flow comes in, but I'm doing what I love…every day. Most people can't say that. There are pros and cons, but I wouldn't have it any other way. New York and God have been extremely kind since I landed here. I've worked consistently."

When I told Rickey I was working on this book over dinner during the pandemic and asked him for a message worth sharing, he said in his jovial, assertive manner: "First thing that comes to mind is self-worth. I hate to use the word, 'complete', but within themselves, everything they need, they already have, and they need to magnify it and focus in on that. You have really found your niche, using different facets of your platform to relate to people. Fucker, you found it, man! Yes, you're doing that because you're Twany, you are Magic, I got it!"

I couldn't argue with him.

Rosie Lani Fiedelman, or "Crrrricket," as I affectionately call her, was my dance partner in *In the Heights*. She has contagious energy and extraordinary talent. She grew up in Breckenridge, Colorado, and started dancing at age seven. She attended school at the Alvin Ailey Fordham University BFA program and went on to dance with the acclaimed Jennifer Muller/The Works for a decade. We have remained steadfast friends since day one, which is pretty rare when you're doing shows.

In her words: "'Best friends forever' is not necessarily true or as true as you think it is at first. Antuan, Rickey, Javier and I, it is true—we're that close. It was a stressful time between Off Broadway and on Broadway and it was our Broadway debut for a lot of us. There was never a time I didn't feel comfortable talking about something because there is never judgment, just support. And we all didn't start out communicating this well. Over time, the trust we gained from each other. We can ask for help. Sometimes I forget how special that is."

I have come to learn that friends really are the gateway for the change you want to see in yourself and in the world. They push you when you don't think you have another drop of blood to give. I had fulfilled my dream of dancing on Broadway, but I had a great deal to learn about relationships and most importantly, self-love. More tests were coming.

When I returned to New York from tour, my roommate and best friend from college, Neil, informed me that he had been going to therapy. He told me how helpful it was for him and was strongly encouraging me to go myself, or at the very least to call and make an appointment for an initial intake. The name of the center was the Crime Victims Treatment Center (CVTC). He wasn't the first person I'd heard talk about the CVTC. Another friend, "A," had sat me down to tell me how transformative and life-changing it had been for him. The three of us had more in common than meeting in college while studying dance and musical theatre. We were each sexually abused as little boys. It was a truth we'd share with each other in our small college town of Springfield, Missouri years before any of us would get to New York. "A" would be the first to find help at the CVTC after he reached out to The Actor's Fund, who directed him there.

CHAPTER 11

The Ritual of Antwan

"The pain passes, but the beauty remains."
—Auguste Renoir

Now you know more about me. You know that for over a decade, I believed that my greatest value was what I had to offer physically, and I used it to my advantage whenever I needed. Before I knew what intimacy was, I knew what sex was, or at least a version of it and in order to protect myself I learned how to manipulate men in order to have control. At a young age, control and choice was taken away from me by people I trusted and when that happened, I promised myself that no man would ever have control over my body again. It worked for a while but the energy to hold onto control was tiring. I wanted a deeper connection with someone. I made a new promise to myself that I wouldn't lead with sex with the next man I was interested in dating. The next step would be to find someone I could have more of an emotional connection with.

I signed up on Match.com and paid for a six-month membership. Within the first month, I matched with "DR," and we quickly found out that we had a mutual friend. He actually called that friend to ask about me and after getting what I'll guess was a glowing recommendation from her, he asked me on a date.

Our first date, scheduled for only a couple of hours, lasted more than five. We met in Central Park, at Strawberry Field, and talked. I remember, just before we got up to keep walking, one of us asked if it would be okay to kiss the other and the answer was "yes." He was currently playing volleyball and tennis in a LGBTQIA+ sports league and was heading to meet teammates for drinks and asked if I'd like to join. I said yes. It was a great first date and we agreed to see each other again. We'd go on several more dates and in time, start a relationship.

I was so happy to find a man like him and when I told him that I wasn't in a hurry to have sex, he told me he felt the same way. The universe was really listening. And it does, dammit! Three months after we had our first date we were back at my apartment, in my room making out and before any clothes would come off, he stopped. I wasn't looking to rush into anything, but I definitely didn't think that three months was too soon to at least see each other naked. I had to remind myself not to take it personally and that I wanted to have a more intimate relationship this time. I got over my hormones and said goodnight to him. I think I did more making out with him in those months than I ever did with either of my girlfriends in high school!

Sometime after that night, we made plans for me to stay at his place and with some discussion, we decided that it would be the night that we'd have sex for the first time. That night, he would be the first man I would offer myself to, fully, *without fear.* I had never done that before. I wasn't afraid with "DR." In the time we'd spent together I could tell that his interest in me was more than physical. I had spent over a decade learning how to read and manipulate men to get them to do what I wanted, and I was good at detecting false intentions. You have to be good at it when you are the one presenting false intentions in order to survive. This was going to be the first time I could put down my armor, so I did, and it was everything I wanted it to be.

I wanted to feel safe and secure with a man and that night, for the first time in almost a decade, I was. In the weeks that followed, I discovered that what we feel in the moment may not last as long as we want it to.

For almost a decade, I had been starving for the feeling I got that night with "DR" and after knowing it could exist, I wanted more of it. I would try to initiate sex with him, and he wasn't interested for one reason or another. I was working full time, as was he, and since we didn't live together, we had limited time together. What made it more difficult for me was that I was used to getting what I wanted from a man physically. It was how I came to value myself. After several failed attempts, I decided to do what I knew best: take control. I was embarrassed, hurt, vulnerable and afraid. I was also unable to say any of this to "DR." I didn't have the self-awareness to share my feelings with someone else and even if I thought about it, I would have told myself that if I did, I'd only get hurt. That had been my experience in the past. Why would it be any different now?

Having made my decision, I turned on my computer one day, logged into Manhunt.net and started looking for someone to make me feel wanted and desired. I found a guy and we started messaging each other and would eventually plan to meet. The plan was that I would go to his place after I left work, which was still me performing in *In the Heights* on Broadway. That evening, I arrived at the theatre close to 7:30 p.m. for an 8:00 p.m. show and as I was walking up to my dressing room, I got a notification for a voicemail from "DR." Apparently, he knew that I had plans to meet someone that night because the person knew him, knew that we were dating, and they had intentionally set me up. He told me not to go, and then hung up the phone.

I don't remember anything else from that night, not even if I was onstage or not. Panic and fear flooded my body like water filling a bathtub. I would try, in vain, to text and call him in the days that followed and eventually he answered one of my calls. To my astonishment, he apologized to me. He apologized for being busy and not spending enough time with me. Each word made me feel sick to my stomach because I knew that none of those were the reasons for me doing what I did. The reason was that I was in love with him, and I was too scared to tell him. He was only the second relationship in ten years where I would fully give myself to a man physically and as much as I knew that I was ready for it mentally, I was not at all ready emotionally.

Our relationship ended.

Years later, I saw him around New York a few times and when I did, my heart skipped a beat. We said hello and asked how the other had been and then went on our way.

I realized I had an emotional deficit, which ruined that relationship. All I had learned at the age of fourteen became how I interacted with men, and when I got to a place where I was fully interested in men, I used that twisted model. I had masterfully crafted this façade of openness so I could say and do very little for a man to think things were going well between us. I did that because I felt I had power. If I knew someone was more invested in me emotionally, then I knew I was in control, safe. Control was "safety." I feigned vulnerability to gain power.

Today, as in the past several years, my expression and the way in which I share vulnerability is not to feign anything or gain power. Vulnerability is a big theme in my story. I'm also well-aware that not every man talks about it freely. Does vulnerability have a place in your story? I know firsthand; you cannot truly love yourself or anyone else without it.

After blowing up what was, at the time, the most intimate relationship I'd had as an adult, I started to do some soul searching. I needed to know why I reacted the way I did. I started to ask myself questions, even going so far as to call my dad to ask him why he had cheated on my mom so many years ago. I thought that maybe the apple didn't fall too far from the tree and that I'd get insight. He was very honest in his answer, which was that he cheated because he "knew he could." He knew that it didn't make what he did right, but that was his truth.

After spending a lot of time in my own head with this, I finally decided to call the CVTC and schedule an intake appointment. You should know that the Crime Victims Treatment Center helps about 1,100 individuals every year. That is, 1,100 souls. I was either going to be among the thriving ones, or likely hit rock bottom. I couldn't see living with this emotional gap any longer. Could I ever experience this thing called true love, the stuff of fantasy and other kinds of "magic" or would it bypass this soul?

What I remember from that day is sitting in an office across from someone and them asking me why I was there and how they could help me. This was my answer: "I've been noticing unhealthy patterns in my relationships with men and after asking all of the questions I can think to ask and not finding the answers I want; I need someone else to start asking the questions."

Know this about the upstanding man behind the intake form. Christopher Bromson, currently the executive director, had started at CVTC twelve years ago. His easeful manner instantly made me feel comfortable. It came with some rich life experience of his own. While attending Baruch College, studying French and studying abroad in Dakar, Senegal, he got connected to CVTC through a *New York Times* reporter who was with Christopher's group for three weeks and found this shelter for victims of child trafficking, which is a significant problem in Senegal, based on the religious system. Families are promised an education under the Koran and the child is then forced to beg and be subjected to physical abuse. The shelter they got hooked up with in a partnership with the UN was ultimately designed to reunite the kids with their families and most of them had no idea what happened to the kid. Some of these kids were four or five, so finding the information to get to the family took a really long time. Christopher was a teacher during that wait period. He ran the medical clinic, too, basic first aid. One kid had cigarette marks all over his back and horrific injuries, but he was one of the happiest, bounciest kids. Christopher remembers the resilience in that kid. He was totally thriving. That was a powerful moment. This was the moment that Christopher knew he wanted to help others. He returned to New York City to work for CVTC.

"It takes a lot for people to make a first call to a place called Crime Victims Treatment Center," he explains. "That's an intense name. By the time they get here, they're ready to dive in because they took the hardest step by making the call. We do our best to make it as comfortable as possible to talk about their histories in trauma. When they come here, there is an expectation that this is going to be hard, painful, and the end result will be beautiful and powerful and transformative. One thing we do immediately and consistently is start to undo that feeling of self-blame. It's comforting to be able to blame yourself a little bit; if you don't do or say that thing again, you won't "get hurt again." But we have no control of others' actions. No one asks to be abused, assaulted or have their trust violated. Part of the work we do is undo that self-blame because it's a hard thing to come to terms with. Letting go of self-blame can be cathartic, healing and terrifying."

I was very hopeful and proud of myself for taking this step. I learned that their services are free of charge and that if I were to be paired with someone, I would have weekly sessions. Fortunately, I got paired with Amie Karp, and our sessions would be life-changing, as they were for Neil and "A."

I feel that Amie's professional opinions are extremely valuable concerning the topic of sexual abuse and healing and simply should not be paraphrased; therefore, she was formally interviewed for this book about our process together with the aim of educating others.

"The main three crimes we see are sexual assault, domestic violence and adult survivors of childhood sexual abuse. I work primarily with survivors of childhood sexual abuse. With the facts of Antuan's history, he was not an outlier in terms of the victimization he experienced. What I can say absolutely is he is a singular pleasure to work with. One of the pleasures of my career is to have gotten to be a part of his work and journey. He is an individual with tremendous capacity. He presented with many hallmarks of the kind of abuse he experienced: difficulty establishing trust and emotional intimacy in relationships, identifying emotional experience as it was coming up and inability to lean into relationships. That's common to sexual trauma. Often, our clients come in when the strategies and defenses they developed that were strategic and brilliant at the time of the abuse are now interfering with their ability to find connection and happiness. Much of the work often is around understanding those defenses and creating a respect and understanding of where they came from—they were protective the time they were developed and stretched into using other strategies at the time of the victimization.

"Antuan was so motivated and had such tremendous capacity to do the work that he immediately welcomed those kinds of challenges. He embraced the possibility of what could be new and different. The modality of therapy I'm most trained in is based in attachment theory. A lot of work is experiential. It's not storytelling. It's the body, mind and moment of what is unfolding in the room and using the platform of therapy to notice what is being experienced. Trust building. Reflecting on it as it's unfolding is one of the ways to change from the therapeutic relationship and then to others. It's super intense because we're doing it right here, right now. Exciting and effective and very challenging. Antuan was so ready and willing. Incredibly active participant in his own healing that many of the challenges that often present for a therapist almost didn't. He was on the road to healing from the jump. One piece that is often necessary in doing work with early sexual abuse is finding a connection to the child that was hurt in the adult body. There are places neuro-biologically that are frozen in the time of the abuse.

"One set of interventions is connecting to the child who sustained those injuries. In our second session—and that is striking because it could take years to get here—we had an experience of Antuan coming into compassionate, loving connection with his younger self and leaping into repairing himself. His open-hearted, compassionate self, offering repair and comfort. This happening quickly was a gift to the treatment and is a hallmark of what makes him so remarkable as a human being. The depth and breadth of his internal emotional connection and ability to go to these places must serve him well as a dancer and performer, too.

Those abilities were there, so it felt like we had everything we needed. We didn't have to do all this excavation to find these places and tools. Now, what do you want to do with it? In relationship to self? Others? Romantic relationship?

"That is what stands out immediately. I was mentioning before him having been an advocate. Every year, we train seventy-five to one hundred volunteers in the community to be crisis counselors and advocates in our emergency department. We have a partnership with a few different hospitals. It's a forty-hour training to go on call for domestic violence or sexual assault presenting in the emergency room. It takes a particular skill set to even want to do that! Be woken up in the middle of the night to go to the emergency room and show up with healing support someone needs in the acute aftermath of an assault. By no stretch do the majority of victims become this kind of advocate. But he did, and he did it in a 'boundary-ed' way to where you're not walking in on this situation, projecting what the reaction might be based on what you went through. To be able to hold your experience as distinct and separate and let it inform how you offer comfort, empathy, support."

To see your life, your pain, laid out by a therapist is a little nerve-racking but so affirming. It helps me consider my own version, having actually lived it, and reminds me of my capabilities to overcome, to triumph.

I learned that the effect of my abuse grew slowly within me, like a deep-rooted weed. As a kid I was a good student, active in first Tae Kwon Do and then theatre. I wasn't interested in drugs or alcohol at all until after I graduated from college, and I didn't have any behavioral issues. That being said, I was so guarded. I reserved most emotions and was so careful about letting others in for fear of being hurt. I remember an acting class that I was taking in college and during an exercise, my professor was giving me notes on my performance. He told me that he could tell that I was internally processing the feelings and emotions of what I was doing, but it wasn't reading on my face. I immediately knew why. I had conditioned myself to hide emotion in my face as a means of protection. As a kid, after my parents separated and it was just me and my mom, there would be times when she'd get upset about something. It could be work, it could be her frustrations with my dad, or even on the off chance that I did something she didn't like. In the moments where she'd be yelling at me her pain and anger towards my dad would be directed at me, and she would say that I looked like him. It was definitely not a compliment, and I knew it. I knew that there was nothing I could say or do to get out of the situation, so I learned to keep my face as blank as possible and wait for her to dismiss me. If I showed any emotion at all, it would only prolong the tongue lashing. I learned that silence was the only way to cope.

Through my sessions, I began to see how I had kept myself silent for so many years, as well as the damage it was doing to me. There was one session in particular that I don't think I'll ever forget. I had been talking about the many times I never spoke up for myself as a kid and how I felt that I was finally finding my voice as an adult. That same week, I was at work and was scheduled to perform. The show started and we all sang the opening number to *In the Heights*. As the show continued, I started to lose my voice. By the end of the show, I had almost no singing voice at all. I freaked out. I'd never lost my voice before and didn't know what was going on. I didn't feel sick, and I didn't have any pain.

Before I left the theatre that night, I talked to my stage manager to inform him what was going on and that I'd be in touch the next day to let him know if I'd be in for work. I woke up the next day and felt no pain. I started to do some vocal exercises, and everything sounded and felt like I was used to, so I planned on going to work. The curtain went up, the music started, and I began singing the opening number and as the song progressed, my voice went out. At this point, I was on the brink of sheer panic.

After informing the stage manager offstage, I left the theatre to go home and rest. A coworker gave me the number of their ear, nose and throat specialist and I made an appointment for the next day. I got to the office and after being asked some routine questions, she began her exam. She tested for any swelling and then gave me a scope, which meant she put a camera down my throat to check for internal inflammation. She told me that my vocal cords looked healthy, with very minimal inflammation, but nothing she would be concerned by. She offered to give me a steroid shot that would allow me to sing, and I declined. I wasn't singing any solos in the show, so I didn't see the need for it.

I left her office just as confused as when I arrived and spent the rest of the day on vocal rest, writing down anything I'd need to say to anyone. I communicated with the stage manager again, giving him an update that I didn't feel ill, so I wanted to come in to work to be onstage, but not sing. The whole reason I was even onstage was because they were down bodies and needed me to fill in and without me there, they might have to make even larger adjustments to the show.

That night, I did a fully lip-synched performance of *In the Heights* on Broadway. It was a very surreal experience, being in front of almost 1,300 people and knowing I'm not making a sound, but hey, the show must go on.

The following week, I saw Amie for a session and informed her about what had been happening at work. She made an observation that made me sit back in my seat. She pointed out that just the week before I had been talking about how I felt I was finally finding my voice as an adult after not expressing it as a kid. I sat with that thought for a while, not knowing any other way to process it. I've experienced many coincidences in my life, but this was the largest by far. It was an anomaly to me. I had no pain, no onset symptoms and it all lasted only a few days and then my voice returned back to normal.

My time over the next several months with Amie would be so enlightening. I didn't realize how much I had pushed below the surface of my consciousness and how much pain and sorrow I was carrying with me every day. I cried more in those months than I have in my entire life, and they were both tears of sorrow and joy. I learned so much about myself. Before therapy, and from the age of eight, I had a very low opinion of myself. I undervalued my strength, intelligence and even my place in this world. As a response to the first incident of sexual abuse when I was eight, I thought of myself as *weak*. I believed that since I wasn't able to speak up and protect myself from what had been done to me, I was weak and powerless. And when the second incident of sexual abuse happened from the ages of fourteen to fifteen, that opinion was confirmed. I think that I carried more anger and judgment towards myself than I did my offenders. I didn't know how to *love myself,* because I didn't really *like myself.* It would be something Amie had said in one of my sessions that would be the break in the clouds that I'd need to start healing the relationship with myself. She asked if I knew what the responses to fear were, as in how do people typically respond when they feel in danger? I told her that they were *fight* or *flight*. She confirmed and then went on to tell me that there is actually a third that most people don't consider and is often the response had. That response is *freeze*. She explained to me that to freeze is just as valid a response as the others and that it was my body's way of protecting itself. Until she said that, I had never considered my reaction of freezing to be a method of protection. I had talked myself into believing that only someone too weak to fight or flee would freeze.

Take note—this is how powerful your mind is! You create your story and actually live it. Why else would I live life every day thinking of myself as weak, defenseless and unworthy of love?

Hearing that began a domino effect of healing over twenty years of scar tissue. In one of the sessions, she asked me to imagine my eight-year-old self. She then asked me what I would say to him. I told him I was sorry for what had happened to him and that it wasn't his fault, and he didn't deserve it. I thanked him for protecting us when we needed it the most, even if he didn't think he did a good enough job. I told him that he didn't have to keep protecting us anymore because I was there to take care of him now.

As I sat in the chair in her office, with my eyes closed having this conversation with my eight-year-old self, tears flowed down my face. I began to hug myself. I hugged the eight-year-old me for who he was. I hugged the thirty-year-old me for who I'd become. I sobbed for minutes while Amie sat respectfully in silence across from me. After I settled myself into the space I was in, I felt such a relief. My entire body was relaxed. In those few minutes, I had let go of so many years of doubt, shame, anger, fear and even love. For all of the negative I held against myself, I held just as much love from myself. That afternoon, I let it all out. Earlier, I mentioned that the effect of my abuse grew slowly within me, like a deep-rooted weed. That weed would be excavated out of me and replaced with a seed. A seed of *LOVE* that I set out to carry forever.

On what seemed like a week of no particular significance, the cast and crew were called into the theatre early before an evening show for a company meeting. I didn't have any idea what it was and hadn't heard any whispers about what it could be either. With our stage manager in front of us, we all listened as he announced that the show would be closing the following January. There were several different responses among us, ranging from confirmation to disbelief. Mine was somewhere in the middle. The announcement of the show closing didn't exactly make sense to many of us because the audiences were full and the response to the show was still exciting. This would be the first show I'd done where the cast was notified of the closing date ahead of time. In every other show I'd done before I knew when the show would end from the beginning, because they were all limited engagements. *In the Heights* was open-ended, meaning it would stay open as long as ticket sales were at a favorable and profitable level for the producers. The show getting its closing notice would signal that it was no longer profitable for the producers.

Let me clarify that the show had been extremely successful, so much so that the lead producers were able to recoup their full investments of $10 million from the show within the first ten months of its opening on Broadway. And considering 80 percent of Broadway shows don't recoup their costs, to have a show do it in its first ten months of opening is quite a feat.

After getting that somber news, we all made our way to our dressing rooms to get ready for a show that would start in thirty minutes. We'd all have to collect ourselves emotionally so we could walk out on that stage and perform for an audience of 1,319, most who would be seeing the show for the first time ever. This was a moment when the phrase "the show must go on" truly applied.

Two months later, as the final show approached, I was still a vacation swing, filling in as needed, and there on a weekly basis. However, I was not asked to perform during the final week of shows, which was a grave disappointment. Still, the producers invited any alumni of the Broadway production back to see the final show and that was a gift I did not anticipate.

I started to reflect on my experience over the past several years. My journey with *In the Heights* had started when I went to an open call audition in 2007, so nervous that I wouldn't be able to execute the hip hop and salsa choreography in the show. Then, almost four years later, after traveling across the country performing it, I would be back in New York seeing the show as an audience member again. If that wasn't a full circle moment, I don't know what would be. I was genuinely happy to be in the audience for the last performance, too. I joined the show as a fan, and I'd be leaving it as a part of its family.

Working in a group of people with differing ages has always been a part of my career fabric and it is where I've learned so much. This experience was no different. Being able to work with people that have more experience than me has been at my foundation. I think it is what has kept me in this business for more than twenty years. I've been able to see how someone can create a career of longevity. I was also able to see how you can be rewarded when you continue to show up for the work.

One of the actors, "BC," had told me that she was terrified to audition for the show at all and wasn't going to. The only thing that pushed her to do it was that she wanted to be an example to her daughters to show them how important it is to go for the things you want, even when you are terrified. She had been working professionally for years, had the experience and the talent and still she had doubts. "BC" was hired as an offstage standby and during her time with the show she would play the roles of "Abuela Claudia," "Daniella," and "Camilla Rosario." She embodied each character so well and brought so much to each of them that it would seem unbelievable that there was a day she considered not auditioning for the show.

Another moment that will stay with me for as long as I can remember is when I was onstage, and my character worked in the dispatch office that was owned by "Kevin" and "Camilla." A scene would have just ended that included the character "Abuela Claudia," played by "OM." After the scene ended, "Abuela Claudia" would stand up from the "stoop" she'd been sitting on and then go into the "apartment building" where she lived. For some reason, I decided to watch her as she did this and in the thirty seconds it took her to exit the stage, I learned one of the most important lessons I think I've ever learned in acting. *Follow-through.* As "OM" made her exit as the wise and sage mother of the neighborhood, she did so fully immersed in her character. Her physicality reflected the years of fight, struggle and time that had passed for her, and it wouldn't be until she stepped off of the set, in a dark corner where no one from the audience could see her, that she became herself and no longer "Abuela Claudia." It would have been so easy for her to have abandoned that physicality much sooner than she did, but she didn't. My thought is that she did it for as long as she did because she was committed to being in the world of the play until she wasn't in the world of the play and that wouldn't happen until she was literally in the wing and no longer on the set. What I learned from those thirty seconds was that it doesn't matter where you are onstage or if you think people are watching you or not. What matters is how you value your own contribution to the work you're doing. It would forever change how I thought of myself as an actor and performer.

Closing night would finally arrive and I'd go to the theatre, all dressed up and excited to see, for the last time, the show that had changed my life. There was a designated section of seats in the orchestra of the audience for all of the alumni of the show to sit, and it must have been thirty people or more. It was special to see faces I hadn't seen in a while, all gathered together. Before the show started, someone passed out small flags of the countries represented in the show: Dominican Republic, Puerto Rico, Mexico and Cuba. I didn't need a genetic connection to any of them to know that I was considered family; my time spent with each person I'd worked with in that show was all the bond I'd need.

The house lights began to dim and with a sold-out audience of 1,319 people, ranging from fans, family and maybe even those who were seeing the show for the first time, the decibel level that was reached in the Richard Rodgers Theatre could've made a bowl of marbles rattle. There was enough energy in that theatre to light a New York City block. It seemed as if each new person that stepped onstage got their own roar of applause. And then out walked Lin-Manuel Miranda, the show's creator and star, who had come back to the show for its final performances. There was nearly a minute of applause and screams before he spoke his first line in the show. In theatre, one minute of silence from the stage can seem like an eternity. He steadied himself as best as he could and took it all in. As the show went on, I laughed, I cried, I cheered, I sang, I reflected, and I felt *pride*. I felt pride for each person on that stage, pride that this show existed to give a face and voice to a group that is not often positively represented in our culture, and pride in knowing that I got to be a part of it.

In the second act of the show, there is a song called "Carnivale" where the neighborhood is being brought together by the salon owner, "Daniella." She's working to remind everyone that even though times are tough, there are still things to celebrate. In the second half of that song the characters begin to raise the flag of their birth countries in celebration and with each one that was sung in praise, people in the audience began to raise their own flags. It was a sea of differences celebrating in unison and it was incredible to witness. As the show came to its close and the cast sang its final note, the lights went out. What followed were flashes from cameras, screams, cheers and applause from the audience and streams of tears running down my face. After the cast took their final bows, Lin took a microphone and began to introduce and call to the stage the offstage crew, orchestra, the alumni in attendance, costume, set and lighting designers. Then out came the producers, music composer, editor, book writer, and finally, the director. Lin's final words: "And if ever you are alone, remember for a time this Broadway was home. Good night, thank you."

Around this time, my seed of love grew inside, transporting me to new and fulfilling places. A friend in Seattle, who goes to an inclusive church, asked me to speak one Sunday. I talked about the word "selfish" and how we have a negative connotation with that, but if the act of being selfish saves your life, why would that be bad? To do so properly serves everyone around you. Selfishly claim your precious time. Selfishly explore what may be holding you back from your achievements, your growth. Selfishly establish boundaries with those you love. Selfishly find the courage to let go of people who don't have your back.

To be in a church setting, no matter how assorted the congregation was, took me back in time and examining my relationship with my mother.

I had stopped shadowing who I was for her. I used to have the mama's boy syndrome, that I could never disagree with her or displease her. I thought compliance meant respect, and difference meant disrespect.

My volunteer work with a New York-based organization called Live Out Loud (LOL) offered a needed push out of those shadows I'd been living in as a gay man. Live Out Loud is dedicated to inspiring and empowering LGBTQIA+ youth by connecting them with successful LGBTQIA+ professionals in their community. I got connected to them via a concert that my Neil had put on. I started by helping create and write curriculums that would be given to New York public schools with GSA/QSA groups. And after asking to work more directly with the students, I became a role model, going into schools to meet with the groups and discuss various topics that focus on LGBTQIA+ issues, awareness, and action.

At this time, I was also preparing for The Homecoming Project, a program LOL sponsors. For the project, I'd go back to my hometown high school and with some help from the school, I'd either speak to the student body, their own GSA/QSA, or anyone that would be interested.

I had contacted the school, and to my surprise, found out that they had their own GSA/QSA, something that did not exist while I was a student. It was decided that I'd speak to members of the GSA, the Young Democrats and students interested in theatre. I was asked by LOL if I'd be willing to make a "day in the life" video as a part of my Homecoming Project and I agreed. I borrowed a portable video camera from a friend of mine that works in TV and started getting footage. One day in particular, I had an audition in the morning and then a rehearsal for a benefit that afternoon. I shared my morning routine, my travel to the audition, as well as the holding room, which is where we all wait, stretch, fill out our audition cards, mentally prepare and chat with each other until we are called, up to thirty at a time, to be taken to a larger room to dance. After giving the footage to my friend, he edited it, added music and gave me a complete copy to show LOL. They were so impressed with the video that they asked me to make a series of them leading up to my Homecoming Project, as well as a recap of how it went. They hoped to use it on their website. I agreed and kept making videos.

With a new year on the calendar and the date for my Homecoming Project with LOL getting closer, I was fine tuning what I'd be sharing with the students. I was also getting more and more nervous. I hadn't been home in over a year and the last time I even saw my mom was during our hour-long drive to the airport in KC almost two years prior. I didn't go back home to visit very often and that was intentional. I had spent the last decade creating my own adult life, one that allowed me to be who I wanted to be, not the son she expected me to be. Since graduating college I'd only go back home a few times and each time I did it was because work took me there. I was almost thirty-two years old and going back to my mothers' house felt like having to go back into the closet. I knew that all of me wouldn't be welcomed. Going back to speak to high school students, at my high school, in my hometown as an openly gay role model was the easy part. The hard part was telling my mom why I was coming back. My best friend from childhood, Sis, still lived there with her husband and three kids and I knew that I could stay with her anytime I wanted, but I knew that this would be a time where I'd have to stay with my mom. I was going to be home for a week, and I would have felt guilty not staying with her at all.

I informed my mom why I was coming back, and her lack of reaction spoke volumes to her discomfort.

As I've gotten older, I've found my own faith, but back then, I was still just as nervous to tell my mom about the Homecoming Project as I was when I first told her that I was gay.

I was older now, living my own life in New York and I'd also done so much work in therapy, so I knew that I'd be okay with however things played out. I decided to focus my attention on why I was back home, not the reasons I didn't want to be there. With some other family knowing I'd be in town I planned for them to meet at my mom's house so we could all spend time together. We were sitting in the living room talking and my aunt asked me why I was back. I knew that my mom hadn't spoken to anyone else in my family about me being gay, and for the briefest of moments I considered giving a vague answer.

I dismissed that idea as quickly as it occurred to me and answered honestly, "I'm in town because I'm doing something called the Homecoming Project with an organization called Live Out Loud. They work to connect LGBTQ youth with openly gay professionals, and I'll be speaking at my high school to a group of students about growing up here and what my life has been like since I left."

This would be how I came out to my aunt and two female cousins. My aunt's response was polite but brief. It was done. I'd spoken my truth. The house didn't cave in on itself. No one fainted.

In the days leading up to me going to my high school, I drove around my hometown to get more footage. It had been so long since I'd been home and every time I came back, there was something new to see. I drove to my elementary and middle schools, to the house we lived in during that time and even through Main Street that still sits nestled in the middle of Blue Springs. So much has grown around it and it still stands. I remembered going to get my driver's license for the first time and wanting a good photo. I told my younger nephew to make a funny face, so I'd have something funny to think about when I took the picture. I drove to the cul-de-sac where Sis and I first met and then reunited after our families had moved away and then back. I had so many happy memories come back to me as I drove around.

It was finally the day I'd speak to the students and just before I'd start, the fire alarm would go off and the school would be evacuated. School had ended shortly before, so it wasn't as large of an evacuation as it could've been. A bird's nest had fallen onto a unit on the roof and caused some smoke. Within ten or fifteen minutes, it was all sorted out and everyone was allowed back inside. I had decided to speak for a portion of the time and also leave time for any questions the students might have. I wasn't exactly sure what question to expect, and to my surprise, very little of it had to do with my sexuality. They were interested about the work I did in musical theatre, where I traveled and what it was like living in New York. That showed me that their generation was far less concerned than mine had been with someone's sexual identity.

After I left, I called Sis to tell her how it went and while we were talking, she said something that has stayed with me. I had told her how hesitant I'd been to come back home since I graduated college, but being back for this visit, everything felt different. I didn't feel like the little boy that I was when I lived here. She said, "You've connected your roots to your wings." She was so right! I had created two lives for myself, the life I had growing up in Blue Springs and the life I was living in New York, and I was very careful about going back to my first life any more than I needed to.

My speech was a striking example of how little weight being gay carries to youths today. Okay, you're gay...*yawn*. What's New York like? What's it like to perform on Broadway? Me being there meant it was more tangible for them to live out their dreams. Social media has opened the door to pictures of world travel and owning a business, speaking on stages, performing. There may be nothing in someone's upbringing that tells them they can do these things, but social media shows possibility. You don't have to be a celebrity to have adventure, travel, or to be who you want to be.

I continued to turn my focus from myself to others. On April 21, 2012, I read a poem at the Crime Victims' Rights Candlelight Vigil. I stayed for the rest of the vigil and was so moved by those that shared their stories of survival. To be in a space with so many people there to support, remember and share themselves was powerful. I cried more than I had in a very long time due to the stories that I heard. This wave of emotions only continued when I spoke at Broadway Unlocked the following night in order to raise money for CVTC.

An individual approached me after I spoke and thanked me for sharing my story because they were not in a place to share their own. Hearing those words, I melted into tears. That exchange was why I said "yes" to speaking, why I started a blog and why I love being a performer. What used to drive my desire to perform was what I was getting out of it, and as I got older and met more people, I noticed that I had an impact on others. I consider that a great responsibility and one that I don't want to squander.

In February of 2014, my father died unexpectedly while I was working on a cruise ship. It happened on a Saturday while I was in the middle of the Atlantic Ocean, with no cell phone service. The ship didn't reach its home port of New York until Sunday morning, when I discovered two voicemails, one from his wife and the other from my half-sister, each of them telling me to call them. My daddy-o was a diabetic and had been on medication to help regulate it. A couple of years prior, he had an issue with his medication and had been hospitalized for a few days, so I thought they were calling me to tell me it had happened again. The morning I got their voicemails also happened to be the day when the Coast Guard would board the ship to check the passports of over

1,000 crew members working on the ship. It was sometime after 7:00 a.m. and as I stood in a long line, slowly inching my way to the front, I called my half-sister to hear her tell me that our father was dead.

Until that moment, I didn't know it was possible for the world to shatter into silence.

As the words sank in, I drifted out of the line and into a corner. What I can remember is her telling me that he died the day before. I'd later hear that he had gone into the hospital just a few days prior because of abdominal pain.

My half-sister told me that they wanted to wait for me to get back home to Kansas City before they started making any funeral plans. I told her I didn't know what he wanted and that I was fine leaving it up to her and his wife and that they could tell me when the service was going to be, and I'd fly in for it.

After I hung up the phone, I got back into line and my mind started to race. I saw my company manager. He asked me what he could do, and in a daze, I just stared at him. I had no idea. But in those moments, if he asked me my name, I wouldn't know that either.

After some conversation, he helped me see that it would be best for me to leave the ship that morning so I would be available to fly home when I needed to. It's not that easy to be granted leave from a cruise ship at a moment's notice, and I still don't know what he did to obtain permission but within a couple of hours, I was walking off the ship with my passport.

I called my mom to tell her. They'd been divorced for nearly twenty years and had been separated several years before that and only spoke periodically. That being said, he had been a love in her life for at least two decades and the news was shocking for her to hear.

I spent the next two weeks off of the ship, some of that time in New York and the rest of it in Kansas City once the funeral arrangements had been made. He died at the age of sixty-eight, much sooner than I would have expected. Our relationship wasn't perfect and for most of my life, it was just above functioning. Things changed for us after I moved to New

York in 2006—in large part to a conversation weeks before my move. In that conversation, I disclosed to him that I'd been sexually abused as a child and that I was gay. It was an aggressive and calculated move on my end. I had been so angry with him for so long about not being in my life the way I would have wanted him to be when I was a kid. I also knew that I didn't want to hold onto that anger any longer. I was giving him a choice. I declared all the truths I didn't think he deserved to know in order for me to see if he'd step up and work to be the father that I wanted him to be. I can't say I fully knew what *that father* looked like. I just knew that I had to do something.

That conversation stands out as the second time I would ever see my father weep in front of me. The first time was when I was about twelve years old, and my mother told him that she wanted a divorce. I was very clear in letting him know that I wanted us to have a better relationship and that he'd also have to do some work in order for that to happen. The next and last eight years of his life were our strongest as father and son. I found my forgiveness with him, and I'd like to think that I was able to help him find his forgiveness in himself. When we talked, it would be open and vulnerable. He could express his regrets as a husband to my mom and a father to his kids and I could hear them from a place of love. I no longer punished him for anything I saw as a mistake or shortcoming.

My father's funeral is only the fourth, maybe fifth I've been to in my life, and it's also been my closest loss. At his funeral there was a portion of the service where friends and family could get up and share thoughts about him. I didn't plan on speaking, but when I was moved to share, I did. I shared how my father had made mistakes in his past, many of which he carried with him until he died. He had deep regrets for the type of father and husband he was when he was younger, which he shared with me on several occasions. Once I was able to forgive him for the choices he had made, I was able to tell him that he had only done as much as he knew to do and that when he knew better, he had done better. For all of the things I may have wanted from him as a child that I didn't get, I can say that the one thing he has given me with abundance is love. My father did not grow up learning how to express love in any direct way, he had to learn it over time. In the last eight years I saw my father grow in his ability to love himself, others and also accept their love. In today's world it is not often that men directly express their love to anyone, let alone to another man, related or not. Now imagine a man raised in the 1950s and the type of social conformity that spawned. That is why I consider my father's expressions of love to be such a gift. I have never had to wonder if he loved me because he never went a conversation without saying it. For a man whose actions for so many years did not always express love, to have him speak it was something wonderful and special to me.

Even with all the love my mother and sisters have for me, there was still a disconnect because I'm gay, though there has been an avalanche of progress recently. When I came out to my father, he said, "I don't understand it, but you are my son and I want you to be happy."

When Jason and I stopped dating, I told my mom and within five seconds, she said, "Maybe this is God's way to show you this isn't the lifestyle for you." I wanted to say, "Can you just be my damn mom for five minutes?!" When I told my dad, he said, "I am so sorry. I know what it's like to not be able to be with someone you love." I didn't need him to understand it; I just needed him to know that I was hurt. And he knew I was hurting. That was so powerful. Even though he never asked about who I was dating, he knew what Jason meant in my life. I could tell he was uncomfortable with certain phrases like "Jason and I are going to dinner" but I could still talk about my life freely. My mother once asked me not to mention Jason's name in conversation. My knee-jerk response as the little boy was to say "yes." Then we hung up the phone, and I thought, *wait, no*! I called her back immediately and said, "I'm going to use his name because he is someone important to me and I want to say his name out of respect." She said, "I think you are disrespecting me." Wow, what a disconnect that was between us.

At the time my dad died in 2014, there was still quite a bit of discord with me and my mom and sisters. I had lost the biggest champion I had of the entirety of me as a person. Who do I even think I can talk to?

There was a fracturing of my vulnerability when he died on February 15.

Then July that same year, I moved out of the apartment I had lived in for seven and a half years with Neil. The lease was up, and I didn't know where I was going. I had found a place, but it wasn't available for two and a half months. One night I was having dinner with a friend and mentioned I didn't know where I was going to live until my new apartment was available. He went on to tell me how he was going to be out of the country for about the same amount of time and would need someone to look in on his apartment while he was gone. To my complete surprise, he offered to sublet his apartment to me at a cost that was far less than he could have gotten from anyone else. I was not only unemployed; I also had almost no savings. I was incredibly thankful for that.

The week before I moved out of that previous apartment, I also ended an almost two-year relationship. When I moved into the sublet, a one bedroom, I shut down emotionally. I didn't want to be vulnerable with anyone. I didn't have the energy to navigate an emotional life. I felt very lost. My parents had been divorced for so long they didn't talk much. My sisters have their own father, and I wasn't close with my dad's other kids. I didn't have anyone to process his death with.

I turned to sex as a coping mechanism. I chose this in the grieving of my father. After it had served its purpose, it was time for me to move forward. This is when I needed Amie and CVTC again. There was all this love I wanted to give someone, but it was blocked by grief. I needed to learn not only how to access it but give it and be comfortable in the giving. I also didn't want to make the same choices I did in the past that were contrary to this feeling and the person I wanted to be in a relationship.

I would retreat into an emotionless cocoon so I wouldn't feel the grief, pain, fear and anger that was inside me. I was a shell of myself, not connected to much. I can remember days in bed watching Netflix or Hulu on my computer and only leaving to get food or to go to the bathroom. I went to auditions, I even booked work and performed, but I wasn't connected in the same way. I was performing as a functioning human being. I used sex as my way of finding intimacy, knowing I didn't want any emotional attachment from anyone, and I wasn't willing to offer it either. That being said, there will always be an emotional attachment when sex is involved, even to the smallest degree and by avoiding it, I wasn't being kind to others or myself.

In June of 2015, one year and four months after my father died, I decided to go back to therapy. I knew that I had been grieving and was ready to move forward. I made an appointment with Amie and walked into her office ready to work.

Sitting in Amie's office again, she asked me what had been going on in my life. After catching her up I told her that I felt as if I was standing in the middle of every natural storm you could imagine, without being able to see any light. I had never been in such a dark place emotionally and knew that I needed help out of it. I wanted to reconnect with the feeling of vulnerability that I'd shut off for the past year. The road out of it was one of the more emotionally uncomfortable things I've done in my life and what kept me going was knowing that where I'd get to would be much better than where I currently was.

In a journal entry from July 2015, I wrote, "I don't yet believe that I am worthy of love and belonging in just an emotional sense, I still want it justified/reinforced through physical intimacy. I feel so inadequate and juvenile. I want to hide." And in the same journal entry, only one paragraph later, I wrote, "The empowering reminder that I took away from todays' therapy session is this; I am LEARNING to walk towards a new emotional path. There is no need to leap to it. Have compassion for the journey I am taking to be the person I know that I can be."

Those two passages are great examples of how I would feel over the next several months as I navigated myself through everything I felt and by November of that year, I would find a new beginning for myself.

I walked into her office and sat down opposite of her with the biggest smile I think I'd had since we started working together. She asked me why I was so happy, and I didn't have an exact cause to tell her. I only knew how to describe how I felt. I had gotten to a place of not only being surrounded by light but feeling it within me. I hadn't felt that in so long and definitely not at the same level as that day. It was where I was hoping to get to, even though I had no set destination.

I discovered so much about myself in those months, things that would allow me to build the emotional foundation I had needed for so long. A foundation set by me, for me. Losing my father showed me how much I depended on other people for my emotional stability and how little I was contributing to it.

Here is another place where Amie's expertise in reviewing the process of therapy and healing from abuse is so invaluable. I hope it helps to shine a light for others as it did me.

"One thing that feels important is the length of treatment. You can't see everyone forever because we would never see anyone new. We run a lot of groups though. We have one who does shamanic journey work and acupuncture. Comprehensive way that feels distinct from others. We're not doing just symptom management. A goal of trauma treatment is a return to pre-trauma functioning. We also know that with anyone with capital T trauma, there is a life history informed by family of origin and systemic oppression. For Antuan, most basically, the arc of his life experience is what one can't help but be inspired by. He came from a platform of enormous injury from many directions. What remained intact in him is this kernel of his core self that he dedicated himself to living from. To not dismiss or avoid this trauma but make use of it as a platform for growth and a lens of how he wants to be, what he wants to put out into the world. It's quite a powerful set of responses to a series of disempowering events."

It's worth noting that in Black culture, therapy is seldom seen as an option and is more often criticized. The notion is to "Give it up to God." As an adult, I've not believed that wholeheartedly. I am a spiritual person and believe that there is some force or energy that exists in this world and that anything that has and will happen in my lifetime was set to happen. I also believe I have a responsibility for how I live in this life that's been given to me. I know that I'm not fully in control and I don't think that I am without control either. Life is not all or nothing—there is more space in the middle than we might think, and I can see how that can be scary. How does someone find comfort in so much grey? My experience is this. Take it one day at a time. It might sound simple and trite, and it's the best answer I have to offer because that has been my personal experience. Trying to anticipate fear and pain for over twenty years was exhausting for me and I didn't know how to do it anymore, until I found a place like the CVTC that could help me. Therapy would offer me a new starting point for my life. It cleared away so much emotional noise that had been present and it made space for me to see and hear me. It also brought me to the most important relationship I'd have, and that was the relationship I have with myself. I would now become the most important priority in my life, not family, friends or work.

CHAPTER 12

CARE Code

"It's the friends you can call up at 4 a.m. that matter."
—MARLENE DIETRICH

IT WOULDN'T BE until 2014, my fifth year of working as a performer in the *Radio City Christmas Spectacular*, that I'd finally get to do the show in New York, at the renowned Radio City Music Hall. I was also living in an apartment that felt more like a home than any place I've lived in as an adult. It made me happy to be in the space every day.

Back then, I shed many tears of gratitude. Gratitude for a nest of friends that I could call on if I needed someone to talk to. Friends that I had for as little as six years and as long as twenty-nine years. My emotional growth journey continued, but what was occurring at that time was a *breakdown*. I use that word very carefully and in its least dramatic form. The breakdown that occurred was that of my old ways of thinking, reacting and being. And with that breakdown came a rebuilding of my emotional self that would be a truer representation of the person that had been waiting to come out. I was in the midst of the most uncomfortable emotional transformation that I had experienced in my adult life.

I was having dinner with two dear friends and in trying to share with them what was going on with me, I found myself at a loss for words to adequately explain what I was feeling. Looking at that evening now, I see it as yet another step on this path of vulnerability that I have embarked upon. Because of their love for me, I was able to express what I could and at times they helped to fill in some of the spaces that were there for me. These particular friends were a source of support for me in the darkest of times, which was when my father died and, in my heart, I knew that they would do so much for me. Even with that knowledge, I still had so much reservation about sharing with them the rawness of what I had been feeling. As I allowed my uncertainty, fear, shame and sadness to flood out of me, they did exactly what a soul friend would do. They supported me. They permitted me to be where I was in those moments, they listened, and they asked questions.

I knew the fear that I had about reaching out to others was not mine alone. The fear was that once I showed someone that emotionally naked part of me, they would reject it. That rejection has many faces, too. It could be dismissive, lacking understanding as well as the willingness to understand, or be that of ridicule. As my emotions spilled out of me, I made a statement about wanting to have one person in my life that I can go to when I want/need emotional support without having to call on it. I wanted a lover/husband/life partner who would be willing to accept and love the part of me that needs to be emotionally supported by another.

To that, my friend said: "Until you have it, that's what you have us for."

I can't even explain how much it meant for me to hear her say that. And it proved what I believe to be true about the power that words can hold.

Please do not underestimate the power of your words to anyone. Telling someone that you love that you are willing to be there for them in their time of need could mean the world to them. I know it has to me! And if you find yourself in my position and in need of someone to reach out to, look at those people in your life that you would do anything for. I feel that our truest soul friends are a natural extension of ourselves and the person or persons that we would drop what we're doing to support at a moment's notice would also do the same for us.

You never know—sometimes they even write roles for you to star in! Such is the case with the exceptional writer, director and public speaking coach, Tricia Brouk.

She had just come off of the success of *Fifty Shades of Fucked Up*, which she wrote, directed, choreographed, and produced at The Triad Theatre. It was a parody musical inspired by the hit book and film *Fifty Shades of Grey*. She'd turn her focus to a new endeavor, still wanting to infuse her style of humor and consciousness. She landed on the idea of mental health. Tricia realized that she had a responsibility to do it right. Mental health is serious. It quickly turned into a social conscious responsibility about how she depicted mental health. And her strategy was brilliant: Tricia chose eight characters who each lived with a different type of mental health. In the 80s, nobody knew what Asperger's was, for example. The same was true for so many other mental health conditions. She knew, perhaps before I did, that I could play three characters and transition in and out of them. We've always had a strong creative chemistry, but there is also a mutual respect, which is absolutely essential for trusting someone enough to push you as a performer. So, she asked me to be in her musical, Committed, and play a character with dissociative identity disorder. Basically, I had to play a mild-mannered man who also believed he was a confident woman, as well as an aggressive, predatory Southern man. It was a creative dream come true!

We both come to the craft of performing and speaking from a place of humility and listening and curiosity. That is how we have always communicated—inside humility, listening, curiosity. How we met is how we have maintained. We laugh a lot, too. She is the first person to ask me to dance in a Speedo, and that's not even the strangest costume I've danced in over the years. The deep connection was trust.

Tricia doesn't have to be the biggest presence or energy in the space because she knows the importance of allowing that for whom or whatever needs to take that space.

Figures in my life like Tricia have helped me realize that friendship and activism can go hand in hand. The pairings are magical. Take actor Javier Muñoz, for example. He is the fire to my cooler approach—and wow, what colorful flames we create.

In his words: "We were emailing back then a lot and texting was not quite a thing. We had a group chain and we both had the sensibility of putting out things that would inspire our fellow cast mates—whether it was happening in the world or internally with us. I look at those days and think that was certainly what would eventually become my platform. I feel it was the same for Antuan. He was cultivating the ideas that he now has manifested. His platform is so inspiring, so nurturing and I think he was doing it back then with those emails.

"I have a handful of friends that I can really, really turn to and share how I'm really feeling in a moment. The kind of things you will only say privately because you don't want to explode in public. Antuan is one of those friends, and we have a group text chain. From time to time, I just get on there and let it out. Then I can go elsewhere and craft something that is helpful to the world instead of just screaming about what we are living through. He is that soundboard. He is there to always receive what I need to get out of my heart, and he is a calming source. Perfect example: A day during the start of this lockdown in New York City, in my previous apartment in Hamilton Heights—notice the name of my apartment showcasing my entire career (*Hamilton, In the Heights*).

"I was pretty terrified. Sirens all the time and friends getting sick, then the bathroom ceiling just collapsed. This giant hole just opened and that meant all these people were coming in. We were at the highest level of anxiety. I turned to the group and Antuan was the first one to say, 'What can you do proactively right now?' He talked me off the ledge and that is the connection we have. Not a lot of people can handle this fire! I'm really passionate about my activism. I take on the opposition."

Life as a performer completely intersects with activism in this day and age. So many musical productions have larger-than-life messages that we are conveying through our expression and performance. The stories in this world can help to create more empathy and healing. How do you feel reading my story? Can you relate? Have you found points of connection, motivation, inspiration?

Javier's story further underscores the intersection of performance and activism: "I was born and raised in Brooklyn. The projects of East New York in the 70s and 80s. This neighborhood had the highest crime rates in the city. Really the projects. Even now when I say I'm from this neighborhood, people from the hood think this is the worst hood. I had to fight for survival a lot and that is built into my being. Coming to my career required that. Training, putting myself through NYU. I met Lin-Manuel Miranda in 2005. Prior to that, in one year, I tested positive for HIV and my parents were both diagnosed with cancer within six months. They are both alive. The three of us needed to rely on each other. I was living in CA at the time and moved back home. I could help them physically and they helped me financially. I had opened up a restaurant as GM and that sucked the life out of me. But it led me to auditioning for *In the Heights*, which I stayed with and developed the character, 'Usnavi', with Lin. Truly a unique experience all on its own, creating this character. There's usually far too much ego to do that. Lin and I are such good friends, we just understand each other and what the goal is."

These good friends would go on to take the world by storm together, not just Broadway, but that incredible story is for a little later.

When I survey my friendships, if I could only paint one picture for you, it would be that of CARE. Four of us have a text thread titled "CARE." It's our initials, and also describes what we do for each other. Pay attention to my three co-stars of CARE, who they are individually and how we come together for each other. Everyone needs a version of CARE in their lives!

Enter **C**hristine LaDuca: "Magic and I have known each other close to fifteen years. In my brain, it's like he has been a part of my adult life in a real way always. We were both in musical theatre and you meet people all the time. Friendships form. What I do recall before becoming like family to each other, is a one-on-one. We were in the Harlem area, Riverside Park, walking around and talking about the business. He was going on a cruise ship. It's my first memory of thinking we were friends. I thought he was like looking into me as we were talking. He has this aura and energy of wanting to know more about you, what makes you tick, what your thoughts are, and he will hear it and absorb it, whether agreeing or disagreeing with it. Without sounding cheesy, I just recall thinking to myself, this person is older than his years. This person is going to be really important in my life. There is no veneer. He is really calm, which is rare with this level of performer. I'm super high-strung. He is always this calming presence. I'm here with you and you don't need to freak out.

"CARE went to Miami on vacation together. We go through the deepest of shit together and it really is a family that was just there one day. I could cry talking about it. Our humanness, and throughout the years, when we've talked about relationships within our foursome, what is fascinating to me is how open and willing he is to be superhuman about his real feeling about not knowing what he doesn't know when it comes to relationships and life. For someone who has such beautiful advice, advice when I want to explode with terror about my love life, career, he has such an awareness about what he can't figure out. He knows what he doesn't know and wants to learn more. He wants to learn and grow. Everybody wants to be able to do that, but he wants to articulate that. We want the people closest to us to look at us in the best light, but he has taught me to own my shit. I've been with my boyfriend for a year and a half, but before I met him, I was struggling with some crazy heartache and vomiting my feelings because I didn't know what to do with them. In the middle of this, I told Antuan, 'you have taught me to own my shit.' I don't have time to talk to the rest of my friends—here is all of my shit, please let me know what you think.

"In this group, also, I'm the one experiencing white privilege and the world is changing so rapidly. I have experienced mistakes, gaffes. I'm a straight white female, but I've been an ally to LGBT, diverse friends—of course, I'm an ally. What do I have to work on? I've had to come to grips with white privilege in this friend group and them loving me. They are experiencing their own shit as black men and women. I don't want to speak for them. It's been a true growing experience for me within our family amidst all this, checking my white privilege at the door, thinking before I speak, which I never worried about until now. It has been a real turning point."

A: Me, of course!

Rickey: "Some of our characteristics are the same. When I first met him, he was energy but detailed, focused energy. He has the ability to get the info and regurgitate it. Who's gonna do it? Magic! He became a brother, one of my closest confidants. Understanding himself as a black man in this world, owning it, stepping into it, has become interesting for me to watch him grow in this manner. The culture and community in which he was raised and to see him now understand the role and/or place in this world has been heartwarming to witness. We are obsessed with constantly pushing ourselves and to understand those in the world around us. We constantly strive for betterment. Hopefully with that, we motivate other people to be the same. We want to be an example. He 'takes responsibility for the energy he puts into the world.' He annoys me because he always sees the positive! It's like now I have to be a better fucking person! I can get to the dark side sometimes. If he doesn't understand something, he takes a step back. He listens to people and really hears what they are saying. He surprises me every day."

Erienne Poole: "I first met Antuan at the closing night of *In the Heights* in Westchester. They had an amazing party and Rickey invited me to come with him. I remember the first impressions of him on stage were, *who is that gorgeous, long-legged brown man*. He was striking to watch as he always stands out when I see him perform. When we were introduced, I was taken back by his genuine beauty, I mean those lashes come on, but also the Zen he brings with him. His laugh catches you off guard, it can be so much larger than you would anticipate from him.

"My favorite memories of Twany are when we went to Miami. It was a CARE trip and it felt like a damn fashion show the whole way. I remember shopping with Twany at this ridiculously expensive store where they gave us champagne while Twany tried on clothes. I kept thinking if I'm going to drink all the champagne, I guess he better buy something and he did to which my pocketbook screamed but he calmly and confidently laid down his card. When we all went out it felt like a spectacle, I always see Twany as put together and cool but in Miami he was large and wild, not like 'girls gone wild' but free and open in a way I don't remember previously.

"Twany and I lived not too far from each other, about ten blocks. One day, a mouse had died in the middle of my kitchen, and he walked those ten blocks to come get it for me. That's just how he is, he will do anything for his friends.

After I finished my first half marathon, Twany came to see me in Orlando and have dinner with me. I was so stoked to have him support me."

I hope this inspires you to seek out your own version of CARE in your life.

CHAPTER 13

Alexander Hamilton and Me

"I think the first duty of society is justice."
—ALEXANDER HAMILTON

WHEN JAVIER MUÑOZ and Lin-Manuel Miranda started the process of constructing *Hamilton*, they couldn't possibly foresee the outcome. According to Javier, they started with six songs, then one act, two acts, then double casting. Javier had reservations about playing "Phillip," he felt too old. Then they found Anthony Ramos. The only part Javier didn't do was the workshop because he was in Oregon at the Shakespeare Festival. He had a wonderful time there, but the formation of *Hamilton* brought him back to New York.

Hamilton tells the story of forgotten American Founding Father Alexander Hamilton and his ascent out of poverty and to power against the backdrop of the American War of Independence. It is a hip-hop musical that has simply had nonstop appeal from theatre and music fans, history buffs, media and critics alike. Being the most expensive show ticket on Broadway to date at an average of $1,000 a seat has not dented ticket sales once in five years and the original cast recording is certified double platinum…very rare for show tunes!

Javier describes his experience playing the title role from July 11,

2016-January 14, 2018: "This kind of work takes a toll on your body, your mind. You need to replenish and heal. *Hamilton* was a life-changing experience, but I needed some recovery time. People who only do straight theatre joke that musical theatre is so easy. I dare you! I dare you to do one show, live in my shoes for twenty-four hours. Only high-performance athletes could understand. I mean, there is no off-season! We get one week of vacation for every six months of work, so let that sit. We are beasts of machines that give ourselves over to this commitment to this art form. It takes your entire life. That is why it was vital for me to have good friends around. I had no life outside of the show. No time, no energy. No social life. I could barely do the stage door intact. There was no spare energy. I had events, galas, concerts, appearances, interviews, everything related to the show. One day, I was rehearsing to perform at Carnegie Hall with Chita Rivera, then getting into a car for Steven Colbert's show, then a show that night. That was one day. It was nuts. Nutty stuff. That didn't leave a lot of space. To have Antuan around, Rickey, who was cast in the show, to have really good friends, was often what got me through. Building the character with Lin gave the nuances, the DNA, so unlike anyone else who played 'Hamilton' after, we had to understand what was happening in each and every line. Every measure of music, there were multiple layers of information happening. Politically, personally, every single measure. The detailed work of that character never stops. I never stopped discovering to the last day, which is unheard of. I've been in roles where I've gotten bored since there was only so much. I was stale. You have to know when you're the stale bread as an actor, reaching the end of discovery. This never happened with *Hamilton*.

"I was in acupuncture, with a trainer five days a week, nutritionist three days a week, voice lessons twice a week, that was all maintenance. It's like football season. Training and staying on your game. This depleted my heart, my spirit. I don't mean it in a negative way, not tragic, but it took all of me to do it. It was thrilling."

My mom had been watching the Tony Awards, and *Hamilton*

opened the show. She didn't know of the show before. Then she wondered to herself, *why isn't my son in it?* When she asked me about it, I said with excitement crackling under my skin, "Believe it or not, I just auditioned!" I was waiting to get the call. Her response was, "Okay! I knew my child should be in that. I'm one of those bragging mothers and everyone is sick and tired of me bragging. I remember the first time I realized they didn't want to hear about my kids. If they were going to jail or getting beat up, they wanted to hear that. I quit sharing."

In the run-up to getting a role as the universal swing, my sister, Robin, told me that I needed to return her life back to her because she had always wanted to be a dancer. She had stopped dancing when MTV was all the rage and entered the U.S. Navy. Having her in the audience of the *Rockettes, Hamilton,* was incredible, but when she brought her daughters as little girls to see me in a show and then told me they were dancing in the aisles, my heart felt like it would burst open and spread love all over.

Robin recalls, "It was beyond dancing. I could feel his gifts of musicality, movement. You could tell it was intentional. You know how you're moved by a song and can feel the sensations. That was my first experience. When he made *Hamilton,* I didn't even have words to explain how I felt or to explain it to people how it was to see my brother be a part of that. It was a phenomenal experience. It was like a rush of anxiety or adrenaline that comes from your chest and through the top of your head. I cried to see him again putting his everything in it and the spirit and the essence of him transferred to the audience. Whether he worked on the cruise ship, *Hamilton,* or at Hersheypark, people would give him gifts or drawings and tell him how much he inspired them. I get it. That is what I feel when I see him perform."

Sis remembers the "Roger Rabbit" and other dances of our time, the same her kids would be mortified to see her doing now. Enter "Lean, Green Air Machine" in sixth grade! She cried throughout *Hamilton.* Her husband, who is more of the sports type than being into musicals, said, "That was awesome!" Finally, a musical he liked.

Hamilton would be an intense fusion of physical work and exhilaration basically nonstop. Needless to say, I would need doses of TV binging with frozen peas all over my legs every chance I got. I had learned, years ago, that someone I worked with had used a bag of ice for their sore muscles and ended up getting frostbite and nerve damage after falling asleep with it on their leg. I used frozen peas because they form where you need them to, you run less of a chance for more injury, and they're cheap. Again, No. 1 tip for muscle aches, along with winding down with loved ones whenever possible, or exhaustion can eat you up.

Javier adds, "The group of friends we are, Antuan, Rickey, Rosie, when we could, we would meet at Hell's Kitchen Bar & Restaurant on 10th. I had a lovely driver. I adored him. The people in these moments have to be comfortable and safe, trusting. That is your connection in those moments. Your dresser, driver, security, agent, PR people, manager, they are your life, so the few friends you can manage to see, that's it. My driver would generously wait while I met them for one hour on Thursdays for a meal and chat. It was my touchstone. I couldn't have gotten through without that. Your friendships through these times are so vital. Antuan was part of my survival. It was so comforting when he was in the building."

The sizzling, sultry Morgan Marcell was steering her role in *Hamilton* also. I had met her in the first national tour of *In the Heights*, so you can see that many of us were selected for *Hamilton*. Our lives will be forever changed by both brain children of Lin-Manuel Miranda. Morgan had worked as an actor and dancer in Los Angeles, and movies were harder to break into. She moved to New York where auditions were happening for numerous projects that she could dance in. Not to mention the opportunity for the self-development she experienced, while navigating all of this opportunity. Eight months later, after dancing on TV, she auditioned for *Hamilton* and was grateful and lucky to make her Broadway debut in that show. She says my brain is like a computer.

Morgan eloquently describes the differences between *Hamilton* and other productions she has done. "*Hamilton* is, to date, the hardest thing

I've ever done physically, mentally. It's also the most rewarding. Two stories that show the top and bottom: I made my Broadway debut and a bit earlier than planned. I went in and my mom and dad flew out the times they knew I would be on. Early in the run, my mom saw the show and did a backstage tour. She stood at the stage door, and I could not get her on the stage because she was bawling her eyes out, like she was injured almost. She was just so proud. Seeing my mom have that reaction and knowing she felt all the sacrifices, the money for the dance lessons, paid off on this night. Seeing that in her face made all my sacrifices—leaving my family, my ninety-five-year-old grandmother who lives in CA as well—for a dream of mine and to be able to share that with someone who made sacrifices for me made it worth it all. My friend took a picture that I will cherish forever. On the contrary, the sacrifice for something that is a masterpiece requires all of your attention and artistic ability. Halfway through, I needed to go to therapy because I was losing my personal sense of self for the show, I was doing nothing else and was drained. I didn't know how to stand up for myself anymore because I was just so involved in the show. I grew a lot. If I was going to rehearsal, I felt vulnerable, weak, had no power. It's not a first-world problem! On Broadway, living your dream takes a lot of sacrifice because you are physically tired and emotionally giving everything you are to someone else's project. There were highs and lows. Meeting all the people and having the exposure I have, now the doors even cracked open because of me doing *Hamilton* is all worth it, but it comes at a cost.

"We call Hamilton a tidal wave—either you get on the board and surf, or you drown. You have to be willing to keep going."

And did I tell you that Morgan is also in the provocative extravaganza that *Moulin Rouge* is? Eight shows a week of pure glitz and grandeur. "It's such a spectacle," she continues. "That taxing show on my body is kind of out of this world. There are a lot of days that I go into work and think, *I just can't do this today*. But meditation and knowing this person next to me in heels and a corset, reminds me I have to show up for this person. And also seeing the show in someone else's eyes helps. With more ethnic backgrounds, it's no longer a line of white women with a token Black person and one Asian. It's mixed and the center point is no longer someone I'm not. Those moments also make the sacrifice worth it. Also, we have all kinds of tricks that get us up and going for the show—sometimes you gotta use all of them!"

Gabriella Sorrentino, swing and dance captain first for the Chicago and now, Broadway company, of *Hamilton*, was auditioning for the show continuously for a year and a half. They hired her as a swing in June of 2016 and we started rehearsing the show on August 1. On the first day of rehearsal, they pulled her aside and asked her to be the female dance captain. She was with the Chicago company for two years as dance captain and has been dance captain for the Broadway company going on two years. She calls it "a lot of brain power and studying your tracks. You need a specific temperament for the job as well, a certain personality because you have to roll with the punches. Sometimes you pick up the wrong prop or go through the wrong exit. You have to go with the flow and know you are there to save the show. The people they have chosen for the show are select, special people. These people become your family. You're spending holidays together. You're part of a unit."

I get asked all the time about my routine as a universal swing as soon as I help people understand what it really is. So, here it is, play by play! When I'm in the shower every morning, except for Mondays, I do simple vocal warmups. Tongue trills, humming and scales, so I know my voice is warm at the beginning of the day and will be ready in the evening. A frustration of being a swing is that people can call out at the last minute. They can be sick, and someone decides they can tough it out, then at the last minute, they realize they can't. At 6:30, my brain is in a different place. Have I eaten dinner? If not, what can I eat before a thirty-minute warmup? It takes thirty-five minutes to get to the theatre. I can't crunch that time anymore because it's New York and I need every minute to get from point A to point B.

The stage manager finds out someone is not doing the show, then I will receive a text that I'm on tonight and for who. For all of us swings for *Hamilton*, we're on the same group text and another may see that I'm on and offer to pick up some food for me.

My process is like clockwork. We have to be in the building by 7:00. I eat dinner by 5:30 and hope to be on the train by 6:00 or 6:15 and to the theatre by 6:30. I live at the 175th stop on the A train. I change out of my street clothes, get into my warmup clothes that live at the theatre, put on music, do rotator cuff and shoulder warmups, depending on who I am dancing for because there may be a lot of lifting. I start with the head and work my way down to legs and hips. There is a lot of damage on my legs. You're jumping a lot and rolling around on the floor. I share a dressing room with seven other swings. We're respectful of each other's space. Then costume time!

We have three or four underlayers of clothing. Dance belt, compression shorts, knee-high socks or tights, the latter of which I prefer. Grips can be sewn into the socks so they can stay up, and knee pads for those slick knee slides you see. Then I go downstairs for the actual costume. It's a step-in jumpsuit that gets zipped and snapped, a vest and boots. Getting dressed is a production in itself.

Some of us circle up in the basement and someone will lead a prayer. By now, it's been forty-five minutes since I've done my warmup. Then a few minutes of calm breathing once the music starts. Show time. At intermission, I snack a little, drink lots of water, and dry off like a boxer because I sweat profusely. When the show ends, it's time to put on ballet boots for warmth. The theatre is always cold when you're not under the lights performing. I get dressed in my street clothes and sign autographs before heading home or out for drinks to decompress. (Or peas and TV.)

In twenty years, I can honestly say that I've only sustained one major injury. I sprained my ankle in an opera workshop performance. My friend teaching it said, "These opera singers don't know how to move. Liven it up!" I livened it up alright—I leaped in the air and came down on my left ankle. It was like taking a plastic cup and crushing it. Thankfully nothing was torn. Being young, in college and feeling invincible, I didn't do the rehabilitation that I needed to do so the injury didn't fully heal. I still do ankle rolls before I get out of bed to help loosen it up.

When I started with *Hamilton*, Eliza and I were rehearsing and the physical trainer came in, pointing out common injuries that performers had already sustained from the show. I paid close attention and incorporated the recommended exercises into my warmup right away. As I was learning each track, I would notice how these injuries may have been sustained in the area that fatigued the most. Man 1 correlates to shoulders and back because of lifting. Even if I skimp on other things for warmup, I target the "man" I have to be as a swing. I love the variety. You have to be fucking phenomenal to be a swing! I'm forty years old and will have turned forty-one by the release of this book. I do not plan to dance as hard as I've danced in any other show, but do I have to?

In your artistic spirit, you know the hard work is worth it. But then to what end? You have to be business-minded, too. You have to be able to ask for certain conditions, and I'm not talking about money. Your stake in a show like this does satisfy the ego, but where does your satisfaction lie as your authentic self?

CHAPTER 14

Soldier of Love

"Learn yourself and love yourself."
—Khoudia Diop

I CONSIDER MYSELF to be a spiritual person, with a belief that there is something out there that is bigger than me, guiding me in the direction I'm meant to be going. As a kid, I would have called that thing, "God," assigning to it all of the attributes and characteristics that are taught in church and depicted on film and TV. As I've gotten older, I've come to learn that I can allow for more interpretations. My faith isn't based on what I can see or touch. It's based on the experiences I've had in my life and being able to evaluate myself, both as I've gone through them and also what that outcome was.

As a kid and even a young adult, I don't think I would have ever considered meeting with an astrologer, given my religious upbringing. If there was a question or problem in life, it was meant to be "taken to God." That could happen in prayer, or by reading the *Bible*. I didn't have any interest in reading the *Bible* in order to find an answer to any of my life's problems, so I was more likely to pray, even if that still didn't completely connect with me. It seemed very ceremonial and ritualistic to me, and I didn't completely enjoy the formality of it.

Over time, I have found my own way of expressing and practicing my faith in a way that allows me to feel supported and comforted and it keeps evolving. That evolution led me to a New York apartment on January 22, 2016, to meet with an astrologer. A woman I would meet for the first time ever and who would share with me how my life was currently looking and could look.

The home office of an astrologer is nothing like you'd imagine or have seen in the movies; at least that wasn't my experience. There were no beaded curtains, lamp shades draped in fabric or candles and incense burning. It was a home that's been lived in, with piles of paper on surface tops, pictures on walls and a cat. It was actually a relief to me that it looked realistic, because it would have been a challenge to have walked into anything other than that. After being let into the apartment by the assistant, I waited in the entryway as they finished a conversation and then I made myself comfortable at the table. She offered me water and went on to tell me how she herself had a water assignment, at the request of her sister. She had a one-gallon water jug and an alarm set to remind her to drink every thirty minutes. She joked that her sister and assistant were "conspiring to make me go to the bathroom a lot."

While we chatted, I was instructed to select fourteen cards from one deck and three from another. She started with the smaller deck of three and explained them to be "...*your guides, the angels that want to work with you.*" As she looked at the first card, she stated that it was *Indigo and Crystal Children, Archangel Metatron.* What that means is that I have a bond with children and am able to help those that are sensitive.

What has been one of the most interesting things for me as I write this book is being able to listen to the recording from my reading and then look at my life to see if there have been experiences that connect to what I learned during it and I'll tell you this—there have been some very powerful connections that have brought tears to my eyes. And as I thought more about what the astrologer said about me having a bond with children and being able to help those that are sensitive, it made me think of one particular experience that I had several years ago. What comes to mind is from September of 2008 when I was a member of the dance company, dre.dance. The artistic directors were Andrew Palermo and Taye Diggs. Earlier that year, I would audition for the dance company at the suggestion of my then professional agent. Having gone to college and earned a BFA in Musical Theatre, I didn't see myself working in a dance company, but there was something in me that decided to say yes to going to the audition. I don't remember how many men were at that audition, but I do know that they were only looking for one and it turned out to be me. After I was hired, rehearsals began for a new work that would highlight children on the autism spectrum. The work premiered in New York and then traveled to Wichita, Kansas to be performed with the dance students from Wichita State University.

While we were in Wichita, we visited Heartspring to work with several children on the autistic spectrum. Heartspring is a leading provider of services and therapies for children with special needs and developmental disabilities. During that morning, we played games with them and taught them dance steps. I remember one little boy got very overwhelmed with everything going on and ran to another smaller room to get away from the larger group. I noticed that someone was missing so I went looking for him and once I found him, I asked him why he was in the room by himself. That day was the first day I'd ever knowingly been in the company of anyone on the spectrum, let alone a small child who might not yet know how to articulate what they were thinking or feeling. I can't remember exactly what was said, but I do remember sitting with him and telling him that it was okay if he didn't want to be with the rest of the group, I just didn't want him to be alone. He didn't ask me to leave, and I was sure to not get too close because I didn't want him to become uncomfortable. We sat for a while, mostly in silence, until he was ready to join the rest of the group. After that, he ran and played with the group until it was time for us to leave. There were even a few times while playing when he would run up to me and ask for a high five, or to see if I'd seen him do something that he was proud of.

That experience is a special one because it taught me a level of patience I didn't know I had before and I admit, a patience that I may not extend as often as I could. I don't know why I felt compelled to offer comfort to that boy. As I said before, I'd never knowingly been in the company of anyone that I knew was on the spectrum, let alone a small child. I had no training either and that situation could have ended in any number of ways that wouldn't have been as pleasant. And until I had the astrology reading, I wouldn't have thought that my own connection with children was any more special than the next person.

Could I be romanticizing a situation in order for it to align with the reading? Absolutely! And why not? As children, we are so creative and can find joy and happiness in some of the most unrelated circumstances and as we get older, we are trained to stop thinking that way. We have to work twice as hard to allow ourselves to see the wonder in our everyday circumstances, as well as being reminded that wonder can even exist.

I tried to exercise a sense of wonder every day from then on. So, when my friend, Tricia, who had recently become the producer of TEDx Lincoln Square, took me to lunch and invited me to be one of her speakers, I started crying. I couldn't believe it. I had just been talking to my therapist about doing more speaking engagements and on a big stage. Tricia just handed this to me on a platter.

For May 2018, the speech I prepared was "Soldier of Love: My Survivor Journey." I couldn't have done it without her specialized coaching. I will never forget her words, which were so powerful, they burrowed under my skin: "You're going to have the impact that you want. Yes, you're in the most famous Broadway musical in the world; however, telling your story about being a survivor and soldier of love is what you are meant to do."

I premiered "Soldier of Love" on Tricia's stage, which was truly an honor. I also did *Committed* again in the New York Theatre Winterfest and later became part of her exclusive speaker community. I always knew that me and Tricia would partner on multiple projects over the long term, but I could have never guessed the magnitude of each initiative.

In that TEDx, I shared my history on a large scale. Several of my friends were in that audience, including Christine, who recalls, "Sitting there as a friend watching that go down and the awe I felt. It's not easy to tell. He did it with such grounded-ness. I've never seen someone have such vulnerability with a grounded sense about them. Total ownership. It's fascinating to see. The story he told, I knew about the sexual molestation, but I experienced it firsthand listening to this speech and getting a new window into him. As performers, seeing friends on stage is nothing new. You're proud of them, but seeing this, him getting up onto a stage and sharing something with the intention of sharing and helping others was a whole new experience. I was nervous as his friend going in. The surprise came when he, through his telling of it, calmed my nerves for him, knowing he was sharing something scary with strangers. He almost calmed me down weirdly enough. He told it in immeasurable craft. The kind of bravery that took."

When it rains, it pours…love, that is.

I met Michael on June 21, 2018, after he sent me a friend request on Facebook. Usually, I ignore those. He was attractive though. We exchanged contact info a week before Pride. I casually asked him what he did. NYPD detective. …*Okay!* He was also on the board of the Gay Officers Action League with activities going on throughout Pride. He said he would be at the Mayor's Pride Ball at Gracie Mansion, which was astounding because I was going to attend as well, with Javier—for the inaugural Javier Muñoz Day! Mayor Bill De Blasio would be declaring the day such and awarding my dear friend as a result of his advocacy for those living with HIV/AIDS.

"Wow!" Mike wrote. "Look for me, I will be in uniform."

The day of the event arrived. I picked up a friend in a friendly Yellow Cab and as we pulled up to Gracie Mansion, we saw a patrol car out front. There were rainbow colored decals all over the car, including the emergency lights and "NYPD" spelled in rainbow colors. After making my way to the back lawn and finding a couple of other friends that were attending, I saw a group of cops standing in a sea of blue on the opposite side of the lawn. As the group shifted, I spotted Mike immediately.

I made my way across the lawn, not realizing he had sent me a text asking me to let him know when I arrived. His back was to me, so I tapped him on his shoulder and as he turned towards me, I said hello with a big smile. As we chatted, he noticed other cops gawking at us, so I introduced him to my friends. We made plans to meet at a bar after the event, he with his friends and me with Rosie. A few days later, we met up at Pride, also with friends in company. After having our first few meetings be group outings, it was time for us to have some private time together. The week that we were supposed to go on a date, I was called to go to Chicago for work.

We rescheduled for a week later, after I'd returned from Chicago, and would have a marvelous date. Then I was called to Chicago again for two months. No bother—Michael texted me, "If one were to fly to Chicago, which airport would one fly into?" He gained a hell of a lot of points for that response. I'd been used to men feeling rejected, like they didn't matter anymore because I had to travel for work. And they would take my schedule as a dead end. Michael did the opposite. I was slightly apprehensive but intrigued. I agreed.

In fact, my friend, Erienne, captures my reaction: "He was always so matter of fact about who he was going out with, never seeking approval from me or CARE. He would say I had a date with so and so and it was good or it's not gonna work out. He knew what he wanted and made it happen. When he began dating Mike it was the same, matter of fact and confident. Then I remember him being in Chicago with *Hamilton* and saying that Mike was going to come visit him and there was a bit more excitement and freedom to his normally rigid but giggly style. I think Mike gave him something the others have not."

We have spent the majority of our relationship in other cities. He works five days a week and gets more paid time off than I do, which allowed him to fly into Chicago early Friday evening, stay through Monday, my day off, and leave early on Tuesday so he could go directly to work. This wonderful man did that for a year and a half.

His own story is rich in culture, identity and growth, with his father being from Ukraine and the family saving enough money to come to New York after Americans freed them from a Nazi war camp. His mother was born in New Jersey and worked for a Jewish family cooking and cleaning. She and Mike's grandmother raised him after splitting from his alcoholic father. Mike picks up the story here: "She sent me away to school. Lower East Side was very different then—crack pipes, buildings burned down, gangs were big, violent crime. Sending me to Rhode Island and this sprawling campus and meeting people from all over the world, like the Bacardis and other families. Culturally, it made me more open to things I had no experience with. I had my first sexual experience with another boy when I was seven. I was never interested in girls. I didn't realize until I was a teenager that I was gay. When I was a teenager later, I lived with my grandmother and helped to take care of her. My father's only living sister speaks Ukrainian. I came out when I was twenty-two. I was never really in the closet. I've always been myself. My mom said it was just a phase and I thought my grandmother was going to kick me out, but she was accepting. I was home on time every day and she cooked for me. My boyfriend at the time would come over."

Mike actually went to bomb school in New Mexico. Who goes to bomb school? He learned blast patterns, how to make bombs and how they detonate. He ended up running two different facilities, with thirty-two vehicles and over 300 employees, radiation and detection equipment, and video cameras for three years. With his computer skills, a panel of chiefs interviewed Mike and gave him the position of highest-ranking officer, detective specialist for the NYPD, where he has been for the last seven years. Needless to say, we don't have dull moments between the careers we have! Most importantly, Mike is involved and outspoken for gay and transgender rights and policies that make a difference, particularly for youth.

My biggest challenge in our relationship has been managing my insecurities and communicating them to him. Early in our relationship, I asked him if he was familiar with the book, *The Five Love Languages*. He wasn't, and then wasted little time finding it and reading it. I'd learn that our primary love languages are opposites, mine being quality time and his, words of affirmation, something that is very low on my personal list. During my twenties, words of affirmation from men meant little to me. I heard very little value in them and thought men used them to achieve their goal of getting my body. Once "I love you" was out there, Mike would say it much more than I would, even though I'd first breathe it into existence for us. I'd soon start to feel as if I weren't saying it enough and that made me very insecure. I also didn't know if my openness and frequency of saying "I love you" would ever match his and knowing the importance to him of hearing it created more pressure for me. To be clear, this was all self-induced and manifested. After mustering enough courage to articulate this to him, he said exactly what I needed to hear, "I'll love you the way I love you and you love me the way you love me, and that is enough for me." Maybe words of affirmation aren't as low on my list as I thought?

My heart continues to evolve into a much better place now with lessons in love and having relationships, according to Neil, who admits to being guarded in letting romance in. He said, "I am partially envious but not in a malicious way. More from the standpoint of I'm very conscious at this point that we only get one life, so we need to commit to whatever path we're gonna take. I've been more committed to goals and business than love. I have a desire to give love and receive love. It's the time and the toll it takes to do that that has kept me from staying on that path because as human beings we are so complex. I admire Antuan for taking that time and really going down that journey. I live vicariously through him as opposed to going through the hard experience of daily demands that relationships ask of us."

In this book, I have shared with you how I went from a person reacting in fear to the life I was living to a person who can react in love to the world I live in. A world that won't always meet us with love. And by sharing my story, I hope to show how each of us is capable of living a whole life. A life where mistakes can exist, where fear is not debilitating and where vulnerability is not a weakness.

Deb Beroset, sassy branding extraordinaire from Chi-Town, instantly got how I could bridge the gap between performer and speaker, and how to profess this as a dynamic brand. I met her through Tricia while she was hosting a Speaker Salon, or showcase of speakers she had trained, in Chicago. The nature of that powerful connection with Deb is reminiscent of who Tricia is.

In what was supposed to be a brief visit to that Speaker Salon, where I'd be an observer, I wound up staying for almost two hours. She says she was "a little in love" with me without even talking with me directly, just in who I was being in the room as a "warm, assuring presence." I take that as a huge compliment. Besides first-class branding, she puts a transformational spin on everything she creates because the work she does is all about the soul and a person's energy and what kind of frequency they vibrate on. In essence, we needed to feel that vibe between each other in order to work on something so central to my life now. As Deb says, "hanging out in the neighborhood of synchronicity on a regular basis—love, harmony, being able to see the gifts of anything, knowing what is outside is created inside. That is magic and here you have a guy named Magic."

I had a lot of fear about creating the website. I was afraid of it being a waste of space, not making sense to anyone else but me and I was afraid that it would be a failure in time, energy and money. I've performed at Radio City Music Hall, a 6,015-seat theatre, and working on this website was scarier than that ever was. Fear isn't a stranger to any of us, we deal with it every day. It can motivate us to move forward, it can paralyze us, it can bring us together and it can isolate us. It can also fool us into believing it's our only option and I know that it's not. There is also love. Love will pick us up when fear knocks us down. Love has saved me from taking my own life. Love has soothed the scars I carry as a survivor of sexual violence. Love is why this site exists. I set out for it to be a place for others to visit so they could feel ENCOURAGED, SEEN, SUPPORTED, SAFE, INSPIRED and LOVED. I wanted this site to add to their joy, not eat away at it.

The fear was knowing I was putting myself out there without the literal song and dance I've made a career out of. Will I have to convince people what this is? Explain how much? It's public and scary. It wasn't just promotion of a show.

Do you ever feel like the world can get a little dark? Kinda scary? Yeah, me too. Together, we can create a world that opens its arms and wraps them around us. Together, we can create a world that feels like anything just might be possible. It all starts with choosing to come from love—choosing to dance with life. #SoldierOfLove

This site now allows me to be a champion of light, love and joy for those that find themselves caught in a cycle of hopelessness and want that to change. By sharing my own experiences, I will show how each of us is capable of living a whole life—a life where mistakes can exist, where fear is not debilitating, and where vulnerability is not a weakness.

So many transformational things have happened since going live with the site. For example, Christopher Bromson became the president of the New York State advisory council. In the bylaws, there needed to be a survivor on the council. He reached out to me without hesitancy. That has propelled me to a higher stage of sharing my story from a view of advocacy. I also presented at the state-wide conference, speaking on issues related to child sexual abuse and crimes of trauma. This was an outstanding complement to my platform. Having a hand in crafting policy affecting survivors? What? Pinch me! What an absolute honor.

I used my platform to improve the system. How powerful is that? The Child Victims Act in New York State that took about thirteen years is big legislative policy. Other things are nuanced and get less public attention, but they fund programs like CVTC and manage compensation to survivors of violence. Those who suffered expenses as a result of the crime are eligible for this compensation, and we worked to minimize barriers to the services. We also inform the office on how to work with survivors of trauma.

To go on and speak to audiences at the SUNY SPECTRUM Conference, United States Merchant Marine Academy, Men's Sexual

Assault Summit Panel, University of Virginia, and others has been a dream come true for this Soldier of Love. Meeting people and sharing stories at these engagements has been a gift. Sometimes the topic is as delicate as a newly bloomed flower.

When I was slated for TEDx and I was going to talk about sexual abuse, I informed my mom to be prepared if this came her way from anyone who saw the talk. I wasn't going to write anything to appease anyone. If and when she heard anything of mine, nothing would be a surprise any longer. I had spoken at a conference in 2017, my first big audience, revolving around sexual violence, and there was Q & A. Someone made a statement that their child had been sexually abused and they were holding a lot of guilt. This sparked me to think about my mom. I never told her that I didn't blame her for anything. That day, I called her and expressed that she wasn't to blame for anything that happened. She did all the right things as a mother. She started crying, confessing that she had been carrying guilt all these years. It never occurred to me that she could have been carrying this guilt. She needed my permission to absolve herself of this. That may have been the most precious conversation between us in years.

In becoming a Soldier of Love and speaker, it's interesting to know that my high school theatre teacher, Kittie Harden, has been teaching public speaking for the past fifteen years. She left the high school environment in my last year. We really do share the same passions. We know that communication as a whole is important these days. She is teaching a generation of students who are charged with solving the most formidable challenges of our lifetime.

Kittie advises: "They have access to so much information, but you have to vet what you read, know your sources and make sure they are credible. I talk to them about their credibility because it's not a given. They have a hard time with the communication aspect. They are technologically advanced, but the spoken word does not come as easily. Their selection of topics is great to see though because they are thinking about issues. The environment, human trafficking. One amazing speaker talked about natural disasters and what you can do to prepare and help in the aftermath. It was a beautifully written speech about helping out your fellow man. That's not something anyone has control over, but you can prepare, and you can react."

CHAPTER 15

Dancing in Your Power

*"To love yourself right now, just as you are, is to give
yourself heaven. Don't wait until you die. If you
wait, you die now. If you love, you live now."*

—ALAN COHEN

SOMETIMES I HAVE to pinch myself. How did this skinny, shy Black kid from small-town Missouri wind up on Broadway stages, speaking in front of captive audiences and writing his first book?

This is where I am now, but it won't be definitive. The next moment will come. The next move may be more transformative. I'll keep dancing. I'll keep moving. Toward impact.

I will dance in my power as long as my spirit moves me. My life is not perfect, and it doesn't have to be. In fact, I don't believe in perfection. However, I do believe that I live a whole life, a life where mistakes can exist, where fear is not debilitating, and vulnerability is not a weakness. Are you sensing the distinction of being *whole*, not perfect? I've put the time in, through therapy, to find and create tools that allow me to be the person I know I can be. I'm not doing it alone either. I have people in my life that support me whenever I need it, and that came from my willingness to be vulnerable with them, even when I was afraid.

Last year, my mom told someone candidly that she had a gay son. This was the first time I heard her speak it. It was magic. She doesn't resist hearing about Mike any longer. Even the normalcy of a phrase like "I figured I didn't hear from you over the weekend because it's your only time with Mike" is like the sun shining. It took her years to get to that place and though it might not be enough for some, it's more than I ever thought I'd get. And in true fashion, my mom and family continue to surprise me. While in Florida in February of 2021, to celebrate my mom's seventy-fifth birthday, my brother-in-law and sister made it a point to express how much they'd like for Mike and I to come for a visit. After my mom heard about it, she added; "I look forward to meeting Mike." WHAT IS HAPPENING AND WHO IS THIS WOMAN?!?!

I'll remind you that nearly ten years ago, this same woman told me she would never want to know anything about my personal life and my sisters had expressed no previous interest either. Since February, Mike has met my mother, both of my sisters, a brother-in-law, some nieces, nephews, an aunt, two cousins and even second cousins. He is the first man I've been in a relationship with to ever meet my family and it all came from them extending an invitation. I'd been hesitant to share my personal life with any of them and with those invitations, they proved to me they can respect and honor my life and relationship. It's not something I've needed for a long time, but something I've wanted and for it to exist without demand is indescribable.

I have had to piece together what a healthy relationship could look like because I didn't grow up seeing one. But I am glad that I've had this self-love journey.

My sister, Robin, has acknowledged that I have chosen to have the courage to make my life transparent so others can relate (especially young people). At fifty-two years old, she has thanked me for teaching her to live her truth and not to let others dictate who she is. I take that as the highest compliment and in naval fashion, salute her, too!

We are all works-in-progress, a sum of our experiences, and never finished. I cannot express to you enough the power we each possess to make our lives how we want them to be. It truly does start with us. I am living proof of it. When I made the conscious choice to change how I wanted my life to be, it responded. We will only get what we desire in life when we are where we need to be emotionally. It won't work any other way. Invest time in your own spirit; it will do more for you than anything else in your life. I became my own Soldier of Love. I learned how to live my life from a place of love, even when I am faced with insurmountable fear.

YOU ARE YOUR GREATEST SOURCE OF LOVE. You are worthy of loving and being loved. You don't have to look to others to find value in you. You carry that value alone as the source. May this find you in good health and spirits.

REFERENCES

Interviews by Author

J. Philip Bassett. Phone interview. July 15, 2020.

Deb Beroset. Phone interview. August 28, 2020.

Christopher Bromson. Phone interview. July 24, 2020.

Tricia Brouk. In-person interview. October 6, 2020.

Bobbie Budgett. Phone interview. July 8, 2020.

Rhonda Cotton. Phone interview. July 8, 2020.

Rosie Lani Fiedelman. Phone interview. July 8, 2020.

Danica Fuimaono. Phone interview. July 22, 2020.

Melissa Gabriel. Phone interview. November 24, 2020.

Kittie Harden. Phone interview. August 4, 2020.

JDH. Phone interview. August 13, 2020.

Amie Karp. Phone interview. July 9, 2020.

Christine LaDuca. Phone interview. August 12, 2020.

Morgan Marcell. Phone interview. August 4, 2020.

Javier Munoz. Phone interview. July 8, 2020.

Eliza Ohman. Written interview. August 26, 2020.

Erienne Poole. Written interview. August 23, 2020.

Robin Rice. August 3, 2020.

Michael Smertiuk. August 25, 2020.

Gabriella Sorrentino. July 23, 2020.

Neil Totton. July 17, 2020.

Rickey Tripp. July 17, 2020.

Amber White. Phone interview. July 15, 2020.

Publications

Brouk, Tricia. *The Influential Voice*. Post Hill Press. April 27, 2021.

Child Victims Act
   https://www.nycbar.org/get-legal-help/article/
   personal-injury-and-accidents/new-york-child-victims-act/

Chmielewski, Dawn. "Lin-Manual Miranda's 'Hamilton' Crashes
   Broadway's Billion-Dollar Club." *Forbes*. June 8, 2020.
   https://www.forbes.com/sites/dawnchmielewski/2020/06/08/
   lin-manuel-mirandas-hamilton-crashes-broadways-billion-dollar-
   club/?sh=563362bc5b3c

Clement, Olivia. "President Obama Offers His Review of *Hamilton*."
   Playbill.
   July 19, 2015.
   https://www.playbill.com/article/
   president-obama-offers-his-review-of-hamilton-com-353545

Crime Victims Treatment Center (CVTC)
   https://www.cvtcnyc.org

Paulson, Michael. "Broadway, Symbol of New York Resilience, Shuts
   Down Amid Virus Threat." *The New York Times*. March 12, 2020.
   https://www.nytimes.com/2020/03/12/theatre/coronavirus-broad-
   way-shutdown.html

Playbill. "How to Tell Broadway From Off-Broadway From..." January
   13, 2019.
   https://www.playbill.com/article/
   how-to-tell-broadway-from-off-broadway-from-com-110450

Yoshida, Emily. "Grammys 2016: Watch Lin Manuel Miranda and the
   cast of Hamilton perform." *The Verge*. February 15, 2016.
   https://www.theverge.com/2016/2/15/11010890/
   hamilton-lin-manuel-miranda-grammys-2016

ABOUT THE AUTHOR

ANTUAN MAGIC RAIMONE is a New York City-based TEDx speaker, performer and advocate. As a childhood sexual abuse survivor, he is using his voice to help those that have not found their own. He is a member of the Office of Victim Services Advisory Council and has given keynotes at the University of Virginia and the SPECTRUM Conference in Albany, NY, as well as the United States Merchant Marine Academy (USMMA). With more than 20 years of professional performance experience, he is currently with the Pulitzer Prize and 11x Tony Award-winning *Hamilton* as a Universal Swing, covering the six male ensemble members for the five U.S. companies. Additional credits include the 4x Tony Award-winning *In the Heights* (Broadway, Off-Broadway and First National Tour—Graffiti Pete U/S, Associate D/C and Vacation Swing), and six years with the *Radio City Christmas Spectacular* (Ensemble). His career as a performer has also allowed him to travel around the world once, visiting six out of the seven continents. Select Regional credits include *Kiss Me Kate* (Bill Calhoun/Lucentio, Paul, D/C), *Hairspray* (Seaweed U/S, Assistant Dir./Chor., D/C), *Sweet Charity* (Big Daddy Brubeck U/S), *Smokey Joe's Café* (Ken Ard), and *Schoolhouse Rock LIVE* (Willis). As an Assistant Choreographer, Antuan worked on the Second National Tour of In the Heights, as well as *The Wizard of Oz,* at both Starlight Theatre and the Fox Theatre. His Assistant Choreography work on *Dreamgirls* at Dallas Theatre Center with Rickey Tripp garnered them the first-ever Irma P. Hall Black Theatre Award for Best Choreography in 2016. He is a member of Actors Equity Association.

Becoming Magic is Antuan's debut as an author. For more info, visit https://www.thesoldieroflove.us.

CPSIA information can be obtained
at www.ICGtesting.com
Printed in the USA
BVHW031154170821
614618BV00004B/55